Shakespeare

At a Glance

Shakespeare
At a Glance

Volume II

William J. Steele

Tynron Press
Scotland

© *William J. Steele, 1990*

First published in 1990 by
Tynron Press
Stenhouse
Thornhill
Dumfriesshire DG3 4LD

ISBN 1 85646 006 1

Cover design by Eric C.H. Yeo
Typeset by Quaser Technology Pte Ltd
Printed in Singapore by Utopia Press

Contents

Foreword

Achievement of Shakespeare

As mentioned in *Shakespeare at a Glance, Vol. I*, the range of Shakespeare's achievement in the field of dramatic literature overshadows that of every playwright. He is the past master in the art of presenting characters that live, move and speak, reflecting all aspects of life in its many features, similar to our own daily lives. The characters he presents in the plays are rounded, fully delineated, entire and capable, and his close insight into what motivates them, his depth of human understanding, his unerring choice of the exact word to describe a character or an emotion, place him supremely above all other dramatists.

The beginning of all knowledge is knowledge of self, the knowledge of the strength of our talents and of our own human weaknesses. Next comes knowledge of our associates, the people we come into contact with in our daily lives — in the family, at school, in business, or at work. It is an essential kind of knowledge, but also the kind that can so easily be overlooked, particularly in the home or at school. It is not easy to come by this knowledge of self and others, but it is the author's opinion that the study of Shakespeare's plays can help.

The plays have a message for each and everyone of us, but to arrive at the message requires application, thought and exploration to probe beneath the outward skin of the character. It is worth the effort. By it we can be brought:

(a) to live our daily lives more fully.
(b) to be more understanding of ourselves.
(c) to be more tolerant in our attitude to other people.
(d) to enjoy the stimulation, the excitement and pleasure of dramatic literature.

(e) to be enriched by the close contact with the mind and the genius of Shakespeare.

The Purpose of *Vol. II*

The purpose of this book is to give the reader further opportunity to delve into another six of Shakespeare's plays, almost at one fell swoop. Its aim is not to discuss every aspect of each play, but rather to give the reader:

(a) the feeling of each play.
(b) an introduction to many of the main characters.
(c) some knowledge of the problems that confronted these characters in their encounter with life.

If this is achieved, it could act as a springboard for the reader to read each of the plays in its entirety, and thereby gain a deeper interest in, and an understanding of, Shakespeare as a dramatic artist. It should be mentioned that the plays in Vol. II are mature plays and accordingly the demands they make on the reader are greater. The reader is, however, assured that the labours spent on understanding these plays are amply rewarding.

W. J. Steele
1990

"God save King Henry, unking'd Richard says."

*photograph on page 1
shows Alan Howard
as King Richard*

A Glance at

RICHARD II

Date of the Play

The play belongs to the early period of Shakespeare's productions, probably written around 1592-94. It deals with a historic time in England, the period 1398-1400, which ended in the deposition of a king.

Play in Outline

Bolingbroke, a crafty, cold, aspiring Duke who later became King Henry IV, charges the Duke of Norfolk for misappropriating military funds and plotting against the life of the Duke of Gloucester.

At first Richard permits them to appear in the lists of Coventry for a trial by combat. He then forbids the contest and banishes Norfolk for life and Bolingbroke for six years.

On the news of his son's banishment, John of Gaunt suffers a severe illness.

The dying Gaunt charges Richard of misrule. His death speech in praise of England is one of the most eloquent speeches ever penned. When old Gaunt dies Richard seizes all his land and property and leaves to go to Ireland to fight the Irish wars. This gives Bolingbroke an opportunity to return from exile to claim his rights.

Richard returns from Ireland to Wales. There he learns that part of his army has dispersed and that Bolingbroke has executed two of his favourites, Bushy and Green. He takes refuge in Flint Castle. Bolingbroke attacks the Castle, captures Richard and takes him to London as a prisoner.

At a meeting of Parliament in Westminster Hall in London, Richard is charged with crimes against the state and forced to abdicate. He is sent to the Tower. Bolingbroke becomes King Henry IV.

Richard is sent from the Tower to Pomfret Castle where he is murdered. The new king promises to make a voyage to the Holy Land to wash the blood of Richard's murder from his guilty hand.

Story of Tragedy

The play unfolds the tragedy of a man not fitted for kingship but flung by circumstances into just such a responsibility.

Richard was an anointed king but through human weakness he proved himself unable to cope with his coronation oaths. His story is not a story of spiritual failure, nor that of a king unable to gain mastery over his own passions which bring about his ruin, but a story of failure in the art of ruling a country.

A Look at King Richard II

He was a credulous, shallow sentimentalist, confronted with political quarrels, surrounded on all sides by a whirling mass of great events. Unfortunately for him, he made the great mistake of allying himself with men who were prepared to sacrifice their country for personal gain.

Richard's Weakness

His willpower was paralysed by his lack of a definite aim. He encounters adversity with sentimental lamentations instead of planned action. He meets misfortune and disasters with mournful moralisations.

It is so easy to condemn him; from a king we expect more. But his weakness is a human weakness, the weakness of the ordinary man, and deserving of our sympathy.

Charm of the Play

(a) It is a play of great speeches, intense poetry and pathos.

(b) It is a wonderful story of a king baited and crushed like an animal by a stronger rival. We are moved by the pathos of a king being forced to abdicate and relinquish his crown, particularly when the speeches of that king are the most mellifluous of all the English kings.

Selection of Memorable Speeches

(1) "Of comfort no man speak"
Act III, Scene ii, lines 144-177.   (Richard)

(2) "What must the King do now?"
Act III, Scene iii, lines 143-175.   (Richard)

(3) "Ay, no; no, ay; for I must nothing be"
Act IV, Scene i, lines 201-222.   (Richard)

(4) "Bring forth these men"
Act III, Scene i, lines 1-30.   (Bolingbroke)

(5) "Methinks I am a prophet new inspir'd"
Act II, Scene i, lines 31-68.   (Gaunt)

Speech 1

"Of comfort no man speak"

Background to the Speech

King Richard has just returned from his expedition in Ireland and is given details of the misfortunes that await him:

(a) His supporters are deserting.

(b) He learns of the growing power of his rival, Bolingbroke.

(c) He learns of the flight of 12,000 fighting Welshmen.

(d) He learns of open rebellion, of the defection of his uncle, the Duke of York, who has now joined forces with Bolingbroke.

Richard's greatest mistake was to place so much reliance on his own abstract idea of the "divine right of kings" as a substitute for personal effort. He foolishly believed that there was a divinity that protected a king from rebellion. He was a fanatic in his belief that he had been appointed by God as king and that nothing could prevail against him. He deluded himself with the idea that the very land itself would guard him from rebels and that

> "This earth have a feeling, and these stones
> Prove armed soldiers, ere her native King
> Shall falter under foul rebellion's arms."

Rebellion in a country demands from a leader, particularly a king-leader, solid capacity for action, self-control and strength of willpower. Bolingbroke possessed these in great measure; Richard II lacked them. In the face of misfortune he showed not a spark of kingly spirit. He became depressed, overwhelmed with his own grief and fully resigned to despair.

Speech 1: "Of comfort no man speak"

KING RICHARD

           of comfort no man speak.
Let's talk of graves, of worms, and epitaphs;
Make dust our paper, and with rainy eyes
Write sorrow on the bosom of the earth.
Let's choose executors and talk of wills;
And yet not so - for what can we bequeath   5
Save our deposed bodies to the ground?
Our lands, our lives, and all, are Bolingbroke's.
And nothing can we call our own but death
And that small model of the barren earth
Which serves as paste and cover to our bones.   10
For God's sake let us sit upon the ground
And tell sad stories of the death of kings:
How some have been depos'd, some slain in war,
Some haunted by the ghosts they have depos'd,   15
Some poison'd by their wives, some sleeping kill'd,
All murder'd - for within the hollow crown
That rounds the mortal temples of a king
Keeps Death his court; and the antic sits,
Scoffing his state and grinning at his pomp;   20
Allowing him a breath, a little scene,
To monarchize, be fear'd, and kill with looks;
Infusing him with self and vain conceit,
As if this flesh which walls about our life
Were brass impregnable; and, humour'd thus,   25
Comes at the last, and with a little pin
Bores through his castle wall, and farewell, king!
Cover your heads, and mock not flesh and blood
With solemn reverence; throw away respect,
Tradition, form, and ceremonious duty;   30
For you have but mistook me all this while.

I live with bread like you, feel want,
Taste grief, need friends: subjected thus,
How can you say to me I am a king?

1   **of graves, of worms, and epitaphs:**
        about graves, the dead, and inscriptions on tombs

2   **Make dust our paper:**
        use the dusty ground as writing paper (on which
        to describe our sorrows)

3-4   **with rainy eyes/Write ... the earth:**
        let our tears of sorrow fall on to the ground

5   **choose executors:**
        appoint those who are to carry out the will of the
        deceased

6-7   **what can we bequeath/Save ... the ground:**
        when we die, all we can leave behind is a corpse

10   **that small model of the barren earth:**
        the shape of the grave that marks the outline of
        our corpse

14   **how some have been depos'd:**
        how some kings have been removed from the
        throne (like Edward II and Henry VI)

15   **Some haunted by the ghosts they have depos'd:**
        for example, Macbeth (by Banquo's ghost)

16   **Some poison'd by their wives:**
        Claudius, the Emperor of Rome, was poisoned by
        his fourth wife Agrippina, the mother of Nero

19-20   **there the antic sits,/Scoffing his state:**
        the court fool (Death) sits there mocking his short-
        lived majesty

23   **Infusing him with self and vain conceit:**
        puffing him up with vanity and self-conceit

24-25   **As if this flesh ... impregnable:**
        as if this body of his were as solid as brass that
        cannot be pierced

25   **and, humour'd thus:**
        having humoured him in this way

28   **Cover your heads and mock not flesh and
        blood:**
        do not take off your hats simply to show respect to
        a king who is only flesh and blood and who will
        one day die

Speech 2

"What must the King do now?"

Background to the Speech

Up to Act II we are given a picture of Richard II as a crafty, insolent and shallow king, who affected the society of frivolous and capering youths, spendthrift minions and flatterers. Such a king does not win our respect nor sympathy.

Now in Act III Scene III the dramatist begins to show Richard in another light in order to win sympathy for him. He presents us with a scene of the two chief characters of the play, Richard and Bolingbroke, meeting face to face at Flint Castle:

(a) We see a Bolingbroke master of the situation but politically shrewd enough in front of the nobles to cloak his real motives:

— He has come, he says, only to claim his hereditary rights.

— He promises to lay down arms.

— He renders all the outward respect due to a fallen monarch.

(b) We see a new Richard. He had allowed himself to be deceived by the flattery of his favourites, but now in front of his conqueror he can probe beneath his rival's ceremony of respect:

— He knows that Bolingbroke desires his abdication.

— He accepts it before his usurper demands it.

— The once aggressive king humbly submits and is prepared to change his kingdom for a little grave.

The spectacle of fallen greatness is always heart-rending. To see a kind humiliated and distressed, deeply moves us. We recall his excellent qualities – his sensibility, his poetic insight and his personal attractiveness. The picture of Richard surrendering his person and his crown to the usurper Bolingbroke pulls at our heartstrings.

Speech 2: "What must the King do now?"

KING RICHARD

"What must the King do now? Must he submit?
The King shall do it. Must he be depos'd?
The King shall be contented. Must he lose
The name of king? A God's name, let it go.
I'll give my jewels for a set of beads,   5
My gorgeous palace for a hermitage,
My gay apparel for an almsman's gown,
My figur'd goblets for a dish of wood,
My sceptre for a palmer's walking staff,
My subjects for a pair of carved saints,   10
And my large kingdom for a little grave,
A little little grave, an obscure grave –
Or I'll be buried in the king's high way,
Some way of common trade, where subjects' feet
May hourly trample on their sovereign's head;   15
For on my heart they tread now whilst I live,
And buried once, why not upon my head?
Aumerle, thou weep'st, my tender-hearted cousin!
We'll make foul weather with despised tears;
Our sighs and they shall lodge the summer corn   20
And make a dearth in this revolting land.
Or shall we play the wantons with our woes
And make some pretty match with shedding tears?
As thus. to drop them still upon one place
Till they have fretted us a pair of graves   25
Within the earth, and, therein laid – there lies
Two kinsmen digg'd their graves with weeping eyes.
Would not this ill do well? Well, well, I see
I talk but idly, and you laugh at me.
Most mighty prince, my Lord Northumberland,   30
What says King Bolingbroke? Will his Majesty

Give Richard leave to live till Richard die?
You make a leg, and Bolingbroke says "ay".

5   **give my jewels for a set of beads:**
     exchange my royal treasures for a rosary (with which
     to say my prayers)

6   **My gorgeous palace for a hermitage:**
     (I will) exchange my beautiful palace for a hermit's
     cell. The Holy Roman Emperor Charles V did this in
     1556

8   **My figur'd goblets for a dish of wood:** my intricately
     wrought drinking cups for a wooden plate

9   **My sceptre for a palmer's walking staff:**
     instead of my royal sceptre I will carry a palm branch
     as a pilgrim in token of my visit to the Holy Land

13   **king's high way:** (busy) main road/highway

20   **Our sighs and they shall lodge the summer corn:**
     our sighs shall dislodge/blow down the ripe corn

21   **make a dearth in this revolting land:**
     cause famine in this land torn by civil war

22   **play the wantons with our woes:**
     treat our sorrows as playthings

23   **make some pretty match with shedding tears:**
     have a rather good competition to see who sheds
     more tears

24   **drop them still upon one place:**
     (referring to the competition) shed tears on to one
     particular spot

25   **Till they have fretted us a pair of graves:**
     till the tears have worn away a pair of graves for us

33   **make a leg:** bend your knee (out of respect to a king) -
     a bitter and perhaps sarcastic comment

Speech 3

"Ay, no; no, ay; for I must nothing be"

Background to the Speech

Richard II's willpower was paralysed by his lack of a definite aim throughout his reign. He dallied over every expedition and encountered adversity with sentimental lamentations instead of planned action. He was partly responsible for his own downfall. When that downfall comes, the meekness of his surrender adds a poignant charm to the abdication.

It is not an ordinary resignation, but a public abdication of a king, humbled to the dust by the results of his own folly and weakness of character.

The beauty of his lamentation in the abdication draws sympathy for Richard and it is important to follow his train of thought in this speech:

(a) He is reluctant to part with his crown but still afraid to keep it.

(b) He shows regrets and tears, fits of hectic passion and smothered majesty.

(c) He toys with his grief and seems to make a luxury of woe itself.

(d) He buries himself in grief and in it finds glad refuge from the sting of self-reproach.

(e) He draws out the agony of his humiliation and feasts his fancy on the pathos of a king being forced by circumstances to relinquish his crown.

(f) The delay releases him from the necessity of manly thought and planned action.

(g) The grief is his own. He is still king of it and no one must prevent him from self-pity.

A man's encounter with adversity should kindle his manhood, but for Richard it simply melts into sentimental pulp, stimulating him to eloquence but not to action. It is this eloquence of rich, pregnant imagery in his speeches that prevents us from growing weary of his lamentations. We listen to him and become aware of the instinct of the poet and a delicacy of mind that arouses our sympathy and compassion for a king who accepts his fate and succumbs without striking a blow in his own defence.

The picture of a Richard bereft of his own crown makes him an object of pity; the picture of a Bolingbroke, crowned with Richard's crown, in turn makes him an object of jealous disaffection.

Speech 3: "Ay, no; no, ay; for I must nothing be"

KING RICHARD

Ay, no; no, ay; for I must nothing be;
Therefore no no, for I resign to thee.
Now mark me how I will undo myself:
I give this heavy weight from off my head,
And this unwieldy sceptre from my hand,
The pride of kingly sway from out my heart;   5
With mine own tears I wash away my balm,
With mine own hands I give away my crown,
With mine own tongue deny my sacred state,
With mine own breath release all duteous oaths.   10
All pomp and majesty I do forswear;
My manors, rents, revenues, I forgo;
My acts, decrees, and statutes, I deny.
God pardon all oaths that are broke to me!
God keep all vows unbroke are made to thee!   15
Make me, that nothing have, with nothing griev'd,
And thou will all pleas'd, that hast all achiev'd.
Long mayst thou live in Richard's seat to sit,
And soon lie Richard in an earthly pit.
God save King Henry, unking'd Richard says,   20
And send him many years of sunshine days!
What more remains?

4   **give this heavy weight from off my head:**
      hand over this burdensome crown

7   **wash away my balm:**
      wash away the oil which anointed me king

10   **release all duteous oaths:**
      surrender all the power and homage due (to me as
      king)

12 **revenues, I forgo:** surrender my entire income

18 **Long mayst thou live in Richard's seat to sit:**
    may you reign on King Richard's throne for a long
    time

Speech 4

"Bring forth these men"

Background to the Speech

To understand the character of King Richard it is helpful to consider the character of Bolingbroke for he has qualities of leadership so lacking in Richard. Many of these qualities can be seen in this speech:

(a) He can act royally. He planned to weed the state of its "caterpillars" and here he is ordering the execution of two of them, Bushy and Green.

(b) He does not dally, but is prompt, decisive and energetic: "Bring forth these men", "See them delivered over to execution and the hand of death".

(c) He is prepared to take upon himself the function of a king in ridding the country of pernicious traitors and does so with natural kingliness and dignity.

(d) He is not yet king but gives orders as if he were.

(e) He had personal reasons for hating Richard's favourites:

— They had heaped personal insults on him.

— They had stolen his property.

— They had caused Richard to misunderstand him and sentence him to banishment.

(f) But he is shrewd enough, and diplomatic enough, in condemning Bushy and Green to death, to follow a course of action that conciliates those still loyal to Richard and his own supporters. He covers up his own personal reasons by calling attention to their crimes:

— The crime of having misled Richard.
— The crime of having brought anxiety and sorrow to Richard's queen.

Speech 4: "Bring forth these men"

BOLINGBROKE

Bring forth these men.
Bushy and Green, I will not vex your souls -
Since presently your souls must part your bodies -
With too much urging your pernicious lives,
For 'twere no charity; yet, to wash your blood   5
From off my hands, here in the view of men
I will unfold some causes of your deaths:
You have misled a prince, a royal king,
A happy gentleman in blood and lineaments,
By you unhappied and disfigured clean;   10
You have in manner with your sinful hours
Made a divorce betwixt his queen and him;
Broke the possession of a royal bed,
And stain'd the beauty of a fair queen's cheeks
With tears drawn from her eyes by your foul wrongs; 15
Myself - a prince by fortune of my birth,
Near to the King in blood, and near in love
Till you did make him misinterpret me -
Have stoop'd my neck under your injuries
And sigh'd my English breath in foreign clouds,   20
Eating the bitter bread of banishment,
Whilst you have fed upon my signories,
Dispark'd my parks and fell'd my forest woods,
From my own windows torn my household coat,
Raz'd out my imprese, leaving me no sign   25
Save men's opinions and my living blood
To show the world I am a gentleman.
This and much more, much more than twice all this,
Condemns you to the death. See them delivered over
To execution and the hand of death.   30

4   **With too much urging your pernicious lives:**
     dwelling too much on your terrible lives

5-6 **to wash your blood/From off my hands:**
     (like Pontius Pilate) to wash my hands clean of the
     guilt of your deaths

9   **A happy gentleman in blood and lineaments:**
     a gentleman fortunate in his (royal) descent and in
     his handsome appearance

10 **By you unhappied and disfigured clean:**
     made unhappy and completely changed from his
     handsome form by you

13 **Broke the possession of a royal bed:**
     separated a royal couple (Richard and his queen)

22 **fed upon my signories:** taken possession of my estates

23 **Dispark'd my parks:**
     broken open the enclosures for my deers

24 **torn my household coat:** removed my coat of arms

25 **Raz'd out my imprese:**
     wiped out the motto from my coat of arms

Speech 5

"Methinks I am a prophet new inspir'd"

Background to the Speech

John of Gaunt is Richard's uncle and it is quite natural that from time to time he should endeavour to advise the king. Gaunt is aware of the danger to the king himself, and to the country.

Instead of acting like a king, Richard had become more like a landlord of England, surrounding himself with a thousand flatterers interested only in self-advancement, and leasing out the land to them as if it were a farm. He looked upon England not as a kingdom demanding his wise and beneficent rule, but as an estate which he could farm out to supply his own personal extravagances. What is more, he was persistently deaf to sober counsel.

Gaunt is now on his deathbed and he makes one final attempt at advising Richard.

The Speech Itself

(a) It is the epitome of the eloquence of patriotism.

(b) In it we hear an echo of the true Elizabethan sense of England's grandeur.

(c) It gives us an image of the dying Gaunt, held up for our admiration as a great patriot filled with concern for the welfare and glory of his country.

(d) Gaunt is here unreservedly sincere and plain-spoken, as he fiercely denounces Richard's offences, highlighting the miserable state of affairs under Richard's rule.

(e) It is a speech full of patriotic fervour.

(f) It is perhaps one of the best loved and best known speeches in the play.

(g) It is packed with information:

— that Richard's misgovernment has plunged a thousand daggers on his head;

— that the ordinary people and the nobles are ready to rebel;

— that conspiracies are already afoot in favour of Bolingbroke;

— that Richard's downfall is imminent.

(h) The courage of Gaunt stands out in contrast to Richard's lack of true patriotic sense and Gaunt himself becomes the representative of England's glorious past.

Footnote to the Speech

In the portrayal of Gaunt, particularly in this speech, Shakespeare has deviated from history, for the sake of the drama. History gives us an entirely different picture of Gaunt – as an ambitious, self-seeking politician, suspected of scheming against the king, an unsuccessful military commander and an unpopular administrator.

Speech 5: "Methinks I am a prophet new inspir'd"

GAUNT

           Methinks I am a prophet new inspir'd,
And thus expiring do foretell of him:
His rash fierce blaze of riot cannot last,
For violent fires soon burn out themselves;
Small showers last long, but sudden storms are short; 5
He tires betimes that spurs too fast betimes;
With eager feeding food doth choke the feeder;
Light vanity, insatiate cormorant,
Consuming means, soon preys upon itself.
This royal throne of kings, this scept'red isle,   10
This earth of majesty, this seat of Mars,
This other Eden, demi-paradise,
This fortress built by Nature for herself,
Against infection and the hand of war,
This happy breed of men, this little world,   15
This precious stone set in the silver sea,
Which serves it in the office of a wall,
Or as a moat defensive to a house,
Against the envy of less happier lands;
This blessed plot, this earth, this realm, this England, 20
This nurse, this teeming womb of royal kings,
Fear'd by their breed, famous by their birth,
Renowned for their deeds as far from home,
For Christian service and true chivalry,
As is the sepulchre in stubborn Jewry   25
Of the world's ransom, blessed Mary's Son;
This land of such dear souls, this dear dear land,
Dear for her reputation through the world,
Is now leas'd out – I die pronouncing it –
Like to a tenement or pelting farm.   30
England, bound in with the triumphant sea,

Whose rocky shore beats back the envious siege
Of wat'ry Neptune, is now bound in with shame,
With inky blots and rotten parchment bonds;
That England, that was wont to conquer others,   35
Hath made a shameful conquest of itself.
Ah, would the scandal vanish with my life,
How happy then were my ensuing death!

6   **he tires betimes that spurs too fast betimes:**
        he who goes too quickly too soon becomes tired

8-9   **insatiate cormorant,/Consuming means:**
        greedy sea-crow wasting its substance

10   **scept'red isle:** king of the islands

11   **earth of majesty**: majestic island

        seat of Mars:
        land of warriors (Mars was the Roman God of
        war)

12   **other Eden, demi-paradise:**
        land like the Garden of Eden, a kind of paradise

13-14   **fortress ... hand of war:**
        England built like a fortress against insurrection
        and invasion

15   **little world:** small island which is a world itself

16-17   **silver sea,/Which serves ... wall:**
        glittering sea which acts as a surrounding barrier,
        protecting England

18   **as a moat defensive to a house:**
        as a wide ditch which gives protection to the walls
        of a castle

19   **Against the envy of less happier lands:**
        against attacks by hostile countries

21   **teeming womb of royal kings:**
      fruitful land which has produced many kings

22   **Fear'd by their breed:**
      feared because of their English origins (famous for
      their valour)

23   **Renowned for their deeds as far from home:**
      refers to the crusades of Richard I and Edward I

25   **stubborn Jewry:**
      the obstinate Jews who refused to accept the teach-
      ings of Jesus

30   **Like to a tenement or pelting farm:**
      in the way a tenement or small farm (is leased out)

32-33 **the envious siege/Of wat'ry Neptune:**
      the pounding of waves ruled by Neptune, God of
      the seas

33-34 **bound ... shame,/With ... parchment bonds:**
      (England) is shamed by the empty charters (of
      land which Richard sold)

38   **happy then were my ensuing death:**
      I would be happy to die

Questions

1.   What is meant by "the divine right of kings"? What
     effect did belief in this have on Richard II as a king and
     as a leader of men?

2.   Read Speeches 1 & 2 and give a character sketch of
     Richard II.

3.   "Adversity stimulated Richard II to eloquence." Select
     the speeches which illustrate this and write an apprecia-
     tion of the phrases and ideas which attract you.

Memorable Lines

I, ii:
            "God's substitute,
His deputy-anointed in His sight."

I, iii:
            "... eagle-winged pride
Of sky-aspiring and ambitious thoughts,
With rival-hating envy."

            "... grief makes one hour ten."

"There is no virtue like necessity."

II, i:
            "... the tongues of dying men
Enforce attention like deep harmony."

II, ii:
            "... lay aside life-harming heaviness
And entertain a cheerful disposition."

"Each substance of a grief hath twenty shadows,
Which shows like grief, but is not so."

"O, full of careful business are his looks!"

"... what a tide of woes
Comes rushing on this woeful land at once!"

"... the task he undertakes
Is numb'ring sands and drinking oceans dry."

II, iii:
            "... your fair discourse hath been sugar,
Making the hard way sweet and delectable."

            "... fiery-red with haste."

"Show me thy humble heart, and not thy knee,
Whose duty is deceivable and false."

"Look on my wrongs with an indifferent eye."

II, iv: "The sun sets weeping in the lowly west,
Witnessing storms to come, woe, and unrest."

III, ii: "This earth shall have a feeling, and these stones
Prove armed soldiers, ere her native King
Shall falter under foul rebellion's arms."

"His treasons will sit blushing in his face."

"Not all the water in the rough rude sea
Can wash the balm off from an anointed king."

"... hearts harder than steel."

V, v: "As thoughts of things divine, are intermix'd
With scruples."

"Think'st thou I'ld make a life of jealousy
... With fresh suspicions."

photograph on page 31
shows Donald Sinder
as Othello

A Glance at

OTHELLO

Date of the Play

Othello was written in or about the year 1604 and belongs to the same period as *Hamlet, Macbeth, Lear* and *Coriolanus*.

Play in Outline

Othello is a Moorish nobleman, a soldier of fortune, a general in the service of the Venetian state. He is a valiant, honourable man, of free and open nature.

He falls in love with Desdemona, the gentle daughter of Brabantio, an innocent, fresh and delicate maiden. They are secretly married, and Iago, a young Venetian, who is outwardly honest and trustworthy, but actually a villain without a conscience, reports the marriage to Brabantio. He feels he has every reason to do so as he has been passed over for promotion by Othello.

The Venetian Senate send Othello to Cyprus to protect the island against the invasion of the Turkish fleet. Desdemona insists on accompanying her husband there. Brabantio is heart-broken and, unknown to himself, sows the first seeds of jealousy in Othello's heart: "She has deceived her father and may thee".

Roderigo is a Venetian and a rejected suitor of Desdemona. Iago's plot begins to take shape: he persuades Roderigo to go with him to Cyprus, promising him the love of Desdemona. In reality the plot is against the noble, unsuspecting Othello. They will all play into the hands of the villain.

A storm batters the Turkish fleet and in Cyprus there is general rejoicing. To keep the merry-making within bounds Othello appoints Cassio officer of the guard. Cassio is a Florentine, a handsome, young, honourable man who has a weakness for wine, women and song. In a chance meeting of Cassio and Desdemona, Iago's nimble brain sees a wonderful opportunity for developing the wicked scheme of his plot: he will use this to stir Othello to jealousy by telling him that Desdemona has been unfaithful.

Cassio drinks too much and fights with Roderigo. Othello reduces him to the ranks. Desdemona, unknown to herself, plays into the hands of the villain Iago: she intercedes with her husband for Cassio's reinstatement as his lieutenant.

Iago injects into Othello's mind and heart the virus of jealousy. He needs some kind of proof to convince Othello. It comes in the shape of a handkerchief which Othello had given to Desdemona as a courting gift. Iago obtains the handkerchief, leaves it in Cassio's room. Cassio gives it to Bianca his mistress to copy. Iago informs Othello that Cassio has the handkerchief. Othello is convinced of his wife's guilt. He swears vengeance upon Desdemona and Cassio.

Othello is recalled from Cyprus and Cassio has been appointed his successor. Iago persuades Roderigo to waylay and kill Cassio.

Othello refuses to believe Desdemona's protestations of her innocence. He smothers her in her bed. He confesses the murder to Emilia, Iago's wife and Emilia reveals the whole truth about the handkerchief, how she gave it to Iago and how he put it to cruel use.

Othello stabs himself and dies with a kiss on the lips of the innocent Desdemona.

Cassio is appointed Lord Governor of Cyprus and his first order is to sentence Iago.

Theme of the Play

The plot of the play deals with one of the most distressing of human emotions - jealousy, and it ends with the murder of a beloved wife and the hero's suicide. But the tragedy is not so much the murder of Desdemona, tragic though that is, but rather the spiritual murder of Othello's soul. From the beginning to end we are deeply involved in the fate that hangs over this man of noble descent, of outstanding character, with a loving, free and open nature and, at the same time, experience the agony of the man as we watch him writhing powerlessly in the snare of jealousy.

Othello is no ordinary vulgar creature of passion: his love for Desdemona is deep and sincere, but the villain of the play, Iago, injects discord into his mind about the possible infidelity of his wife, and the discord acts like a cancer in his soul. Because of this, we see him fall from the ideal heights of a renowned commander of the Venetian army to the terrible, shameful and humiliating depths of deep damnation. We do not only see him fall, we are involved in his spiritual self-destruction.

Sexual jealousy is a passion common to all humanity. We are all liable to blinding jealousy which can destroy us, unless we are on our guard, as it destroyed Othello. Yet the play is not just a sordid tale of sexual jealousy, nor a mere tragedy of low intrigue. It is a play of high tragedy, romantic rather than brutal, and Shakespeare's genius lifts the story from the level of intrigue to one of high drama.

Charm of the Play

The plot is straightforward and simple, and the number of characters small. There is no subplot and the action moves fast from the moment Othello and his wife land in Cyprus, with the tension of the cancer of jealousy mounting all the time until the moment when Othello kills himself.

It is a masterpiece of construction. It may not have:

— the variety, the depth nor the pathos of *Hamlet*

— nor the tremendous power of *King Lear*

—   nor has it the claustrophobic atmosphere of *Macbeth*.

But the play is set on a grand scale: it

—   takes a grip upon our emotions.

—   is more relentless in the tragic progress of its main characters.

—   is more sustained than the other great plays.

—   vividly presents human conflict in tragically dark, abysmal terms.

In other plays of Shakespeare we are spectators of tragedy and the effect can be terrifying, soul-searching. In *Othello*, if we are alert to every verbal suggestion, if we not only hear and see, but use the eyes and ears of our minds:

—   we become totally involved in the tragedy.

—   we want to participate.

—   we want to speak to the characters, to Othello, to Desdemona, to Cassio.

—   we want to advise and warn them of the consequences of their actions.

Background to the Story

The story of the play develops against the background of notable events during the Cyprus wars and, on this backcloth, Shakespeare paints the development of the plot and the characters involved.

Cyprus was subject to the Republic of Venice from 1471. The times were tumultous, with the threat of war ever present. The Turks under Selim II planned to invade Cyprus in 1570 which they did in 1571. They assembled their fleet at Rhodes, sailed to Cyprus, then back to Rhodes, then back again to Cyprus. It was a real threat by the Turkish fleet to the security and prosperity of the bustling commercial Republic of Venice, with the undertones of a threat to a Christian state.

Such a situation and threat demanded an outstanding man at the head of military affairs in Venice. The Duke and Senators found that man in the person of Othello and he at once became indispensable to the military defence of the Venetian Republic.

Outstanding Qualities of Othello

He is the central figure of the play and around him the whole drama revolves. In the first scene of the play we get an unflattering picture of him, but it is a picture painted by Iago who suffers from a rankling sense of injury because Cassio has been appointed to a senior position in the army. Iago feels that he himself merits the promotion and concludes that Othello has simply promoted one of his favourites.

The picture Iago paints is that of a proud, blustering soldier of fortune, a man of no morals, and of unsound judgment. Later on in the play a more realistic picture of his qualities is presented to us:

(a) He is a romantic figure descended from royal lineage.

(b) He is a military leader of men: alert, poised, proud, single-minded in his dedication to duty.

(c) He has a public image of discipline, self-control - a man with a cool head, and firm decision in time of emergency.

(d) His qualities of leadership have been recognised by the Duke and the Senate who see him as a fearless warrior, a man used to command and fit to be a leader.

(c) He is a soldier of great dignity with many military achievements to his credit.

(f) He is an exceptional man, convinced of his own worth to the state and conscious of his own integrity.

(g) He is deeply in love with Desdemona.

Selection of Memorable Speeches

(1) "Thus do I ever make my fool my purse"
      Act I, Scene iii, lines 377-398.   (Iago)

(2) "That Cassio loves her, I do well believe it"
      Act II, Scene i, lines 280-306.   (Iago)

(3) "Think'st thou I'ld make a life of jealousy"
      Act III, Scene iii, lines 177-192.   (Othello)

(4) "This fellow's of exceeding honesty"
      Act III, Scene iii, lines 258-277.   (Othello)

(5) "It is the cause, it is the cause, my soul"
      Act V, Scene ii, lines 1-22.   (Othello)

Speech 1

"Thus do I ever make my fool my purse"

Iago's Character - an Enigma

To understand this soliloquy of Iago we have first of all to try to understand the man. This is a very difficult task indeed:

(a) His character is elusive, enigmatic, constantly changing.

(b) It is complex, puzzling.

(c) He is possibly the greatest stage-villain ever created, and to understand him is an absorbing study.

The difficulty for us is that, he is a man who scorns to make his outward behaviour a true guide to his inner feelings and to know him we must, as it were, probe these inner feelings. We must get to know his secret thoughts and to experience close emotional contact with them. We ought to be able to do that in a soliloquy in which the character opens his mind and his soul to us. But Iago is too clever to allow us to enter his world quickly or easily: he is successful in creating an image of his own straightforwardness, but at the same time creates difficulties for us in distinguishing between fact and fiction. In short, we find it difficult to know for sure whether what he says is true or false.

In analysing his character - in order to give this speech its full impact - the difficulty is that Iago tells us about his opinions, his suspicions and his plans but not about himself. So we are left with a puzzle:

(a) Is he just an ordinary villain, human in his feelings?

(b) Is he just a young, professional soldier, disappointed and chaffing at the promotion of Cassio?

(c) Is his sense of unrewarded merit the real key to his present attitude and his actions in the future?

(d) Is he a relatively decent young man plunging for the first time into dastardly wickedness?

What We Know about Iago

(a) We know he is 28 years of age.

(b) We know he is an "ancient", a standard-bearer in the Venetian army, a subordinate rank.

(c) We know that he has applied for promotion and has been passed over. This embitters him and he feels the sting of his present humble position.

(d) He is rankled by the "curse of service" that permits "preferment" to go by letter and affection, not by the old system of promotion.

(e) He is convinced that he is intellectually superior to those above him and convinced that he has more military experience and better qualifications than Cassio.

(f) He cannot understand how some men are content to serve quietly and honestly and has nothing but contempt for the Christian concept of the ideal servant who sees beauty and dignity in service to others.

(g) When he serves, it will be for his own self-interest. He is prepared to put on the appearance of loyalty to Othello, but does so simply to serve his own peculiar ends.

Shakespeare's Plan

The dramatist sets out not simply to devise an evil character: he had to convince an audience of the reality of his creation. *Othello* is not a tragedy of little people caught up in a story of pettiness but a tragedy of great souls, caught and crushed by a great intellect.

Iago's intellect is piercing, remorseless, devising cruelty of a superhuman type. It can be seen in:

(a) Iago's knowledge of the strengths and weaknesses of his victims: Othello, Desdemona, Cassio, Roderigo.

(b) How it turns Desdemona's virtue into a net to enmesh all the others.

(c) How it grows and grows, allowing no opportunity to slip by and seeing in everything a golden opportunity for furthering the involvement of the characters to be punished by Iago.

(d) How at first it requires a motive of revenge for the furthering of the scheme, how it no longer needs a reason, but becomes totally immersed in the action of evil itself, seeking malicious glee at the turning of goodness to evil.

(e) His intellect knows nothing of emotion: it makes him indifferent to the pain he causes Cassio and indifferent to the torture he inflicts on Othello and Desdemona.

(f) It is an intellect that devises villainy towards others but at the same time keeps his own untarnished reputation of being an honest man.

(g) It is an intellect that demands:

— a willpower strong enough to put into operation what the intellect recommends.

— the faculty of an accomplished liar.

— the expertise of the manipulator of the innocent.

— the skill of handling the plot against his enemies, without betraying himself or becoming less devious in his methods; and all this is with no partner in his abominable schemes - he has to rely solely on his own resources.

— the quick confidence of responding to the needs of the occasion: to be now a jolly companion to Cassio; now a moralist with Montano; now a loyal soldier in the presence of Othello.

A Worthwhile Study

To come to grips with the character of Iago in this speech is a worthwhile study. He is so complex, so devoid of all feeling of moral obligation. In short, Iago's world is a world where:

(a) honour, truth, love, self-sacrifice do not exist.

(b) the only motive of action is self-interest.

(c) the only emotion is one of contempt for those whom he thinks are intellectually inferior to him.

(d) there is hatred of those who oppose his self-centred schemes.

A Glance at His Speech

Now that we have some idea of the character of the man, let us have a glance at his speech. The play is a tragedy of infectious jealousy with several of the characters showing signs of this cancer.

Roderigo's jealousy is that of a man who is ignored by a girl. He fancied himself a suitable suitor for Desdemona, was unsuccessful in his suit and became an easy prey in the hands of Iago.

Bianca's jealousy is a sexual jealousy leading to unlawful liaisons and exploding in spiteful vituperation.

Othello's jealousy will eventually drive him to sacrifice his wife's life and his own.

All these characters are in the hands of Iago, who is himself jealous of Cassio. In this speech we see the beginnings of his plots which result in terrible crimes:

(a)   He declares his hatred of Othello: "I hate the Moor".

(b)   He gives a reason for his hatred: his suspicion that Othello has been intimate with his wife, Emilia - "'twixt my sheets/H'as done my office".

(c)   It is mere suspicion on his part but he is prepared to accept it "for surety", as something that has already happened. The suspicion is like a poison eating into his soul.

(d)   He knows it will not be easy to insinuate his way into the sanctuary of Othello's being where the love for Desdemona is firmly lodged.

(e)   His mind works hard and he sees a solution to his problem: use Othello's high opinion of him - "He holds me well". He knows if he can do this "the better shall my purpose work on him".

(f)   He knows that that is not the end of the problem, only just the beginning and he ponders: how to go about it?

(g)   The mind ticks over and the solution comes easily: use Cassio. He knows Cassio is a handsome man, "a proper man", with "a person and smooth dispose", so attractive as "to make women false".

(h)   But how to use Cassio is another problem. That requires a lot of thought. Again the solution comes: suggest to the Moor that Cassio has been "too familiar with his wife".

(i)   But even here there is difficulty in the way the suggestion is to be made. What will make it less difficult is Othello's character: he is "of a free and open nature".

(j)   The idea of his plan is working out well and he gloats over his success: "I have 't! It is engendered".

(k)   Iago is now convinced that his plan to control the destiny of others is well under way and his victims are unsuspecting. It simply requires his deviously cunning mind to bring the plan to fruition.

(l)   One final thing might help: call up all the tribes of hell and the darkness of night: "Hell and night/Must bring this monstrous birth to the world's light".

Speaking the Speech

As you speak this speech of Iago's, enter into the spirit of the man. Pause to consider each problem that faces him and reflect on each possible solution. Try to imagine the mind of Iago at work, then give the speech its full force as you, with him, gloat over the success of the plan in the final two lines.

Speech 1: "Thus do I ever make my fool my purse"

IAGO

      Thus do I ever make my fool my purse;
For I mine own gained knowledge should profane
If I would time expend with such a snipe
But for my sport and profit. I hate the Moor,
And it is thought abroad that 'twixt my sheets   5
H'as done my office. I know not if 't be true;
But I, for mere suspicion in that kind,
Will do as if for surety. He holds me well;
The better shall my purpose work on him.
Cassio's a proper man. Let me see now: 10
To get his place, and to plume up my will
In double knavery - How, how? - Let's see: -
After some time, to abuse Othello's ears
That he is too familiar with his wife.
He hath a person and a smooth dispose   15
To be suspected - framed to make women false.
The Moor is of a free and open nature
That thinks men honest that but seem to be so;
And will as tenderly be led by th' nose
As asses are.   20
I have't! It is engend'red! Hell and night
Must bring this monstrous birth to the world's light.

1 **Thus do I ever make my fool my purse:**
  in this way I trick my victim and then use him for my own
  ends

2 **mine own gained knowledge:**
  my practical experience of men

3 **If I would expend time with such a snipe:**
  if I spend time with such a fool

5   **it is thought abroad:** it is commonly known

5-6   **'twixt my sheets/H'as done my office**
       he has slept with my wife

7-8   **But I, for mere suspicion ... for surety:**
       I will accept even the slightest suggestion of his miscon-
       duct as being proof that it has already happened

8   **holds me well:** has a high opinion of me

10   **Cassio's a proper man:** Cassio is a handsome man

11   **plume up my will:** gratify my ego

12   **In double knavery:**
      in doing harm to both Othello and Cassio

15   **He hath a person and a smooth dispose:**
      he is an attractive man with a charming manner

16   **To be suspected:** to arouse suspicion

      framed to make women false:
      (Cassio is just the right person to) lead women astray

21   **I have 't! It is engend'red!:**
      the idea is beginning to take shape in my mind

Speech 2

"That Cassio loves her, I do well believe it"

Background to the Speech

As we approach this second soliloquy of Iago's, it is important to sit back for a moment and consider what we know of the story of events so far and observe the mind of this villain still at work, ready to pounce upon every opportunity to further his evil schemes.

(a) We know that Othello and Desdemona have been married secretly in Venice.

(b) We know that Othello has been appointed Commander of the Venetian forces and has been sent to Cyprus as deliverer of the land.

(c) We know that Desdemona has left Venice to join her husband. This is significant: it will make the villain's scheme easier to work; she will be separated from her home and the friends of her youth, depending entirely upon Othello for everything.

(d) We know that the Turkish fleet which was about to attack met with disaster in a devastating storm at sea. This resulted in a period of peace for Cyprus, but a peace that could be disrupted at any moment and one which demanded a watchful security on the island. Cassio as second in-command would be totally responsible for such security and coming within this responsibility would be the preven-tion of drunken brawls or mutiny of the islanders.

Iago's Plan of Action

Iago's villainy is not the growth of a moment: it develops slowly.

It is attentive to every movement of those who fall into his power. We know what his plan is: to displant Cassio and revenge himself on Othello. But it is a plan formulated only in general terms. He has still to decide how to work his revenge into the general framework of his plan. But all seems to be falling into shape for him.

Iago's First Victim

(a) Cassio is a competent soldier who holds Othello in high regard. He looks upon him as a god coming to breathe life-force into Cyprus.

(b) Cassio is also a handsome man of fashion, a polished Florentine gentleman and it is only natural that in welcoming Desdemona to Cyprus he should kiss her hand out of courtesy to her, and also because she is the wife of his Commander.

The warped intellect of Iago sees in these courtesies "a web" to "ensnare as great a fly as Cassio" and a means of stripping him of his "lieutenantry". He will inform Othello about it and slyly point out to him that it was not a mere act of gallantry but rather one of "lechery", a true "index and prologue to the history of lust and foul thoughts".

Iago's Second Victim

Roderigo is already in love with Desdemona and so can become an easy prey. With this in mind Iago sets out to:

(a) make him jealous.

(b) tell him that Desdemona is in love with Cassio, even though that requires destroying Desdemona's character.

(c) If Roderigo is not prepared to accept the idea of the possibility of Desdemona's unfaithfulness, Iago will state as a fact to him that the "woman has found him [Cassio] already". This idea will make him more jealous.

More importantly, Iago uses him as an agent for his evil deeds, encouraging him to inveigle Cassio into a drunken brawl and then to cause mutiny among the islanders. Othello will blame Cassio for disrupting the peace of Cyprus and will degrade him from his rank. Through the agency of his second victim Iago sees his plan taking a firm shape and developing.

Iago's Third Victim

Desdemona who is a "paragon" of all virtues, excelling "the quirks of blazoning pens" and who is deeply in love with Othello, is to be his third victim.

He watched the reunion of the recently-married pair and saw evidence of tenderness and love. That was too much for his suspicious nature. His mind ticked over again and searched for a way round this in order to convince his victims, first of all Roderigo, and then Othello himself. The solution to his problem is to:

(a) suggest that she loved the Moor only for his "bragging" and his "fantastical lies".

(b) emphasise the fact that in years, manners and beauty, the Moor was defective.

(c) stress the point that soon Desdemona will abhor the Moor and will, with fresh appetite, look for for a second choice: "her eye must be fed".

(d) involve Desdemona in pleading for leniency for Cassio, then use this to torture the mind of Othello.

Iago's Main Victim

Othello is to be Iago's main victim. His plan now is to put the Moor into "a jealousy so strong/That judgement cannot cure".

He is determined to destroy the happiness of their reunion and feels justified in doing so. All along he has suspected the Moor of having "leaped into my seat" and being intimate with Emilia. The suspicion gnaws at him and he promises never to be content: "Till I am even with him, wife for wife".

He recognises the difficulty of dealing with Othello: he will not be an easy victim. Therefore, he has to take care to be observant and listen to everything that Othello says:

(a) He sees Othello overjoyed at the reunion with his wife.

(b) He hears the devoted lover and husband use words of tenderness and love, calling Desdemona "O my fair warrior", "my soul's joy", "O my sweet".

(c) He sees that joy is overshadowed by the statement of an ageing, disillusioned man, who is experiencing so much happiness that he fears it will all end soon: "if it were now to die/ 'Tis here, but yet confus'd".

Iago's Character

As we read this soliloquy of Iago's we see the warped intellect of the man at work:

(a) He is setting out to destroy generous lives.

(b) He shows no emotion of respect for his fellowmen.

(c) He is cool, self-disciplined, egocentric.

(d) Other people are only tools in his hands.

(e) He is concocting uses for each of them in his monstrous plan

(f) He despises all of them because he is able to make use of them.

As we read and study this speech, note a few points:

(a) Here we see Iago actually engaged in thinking.

(b) He is choosing, testing each idea and examining it most carefully.

(c)   Yet, like all sinister men, he tells nothing or very little about himself. What he actually is, is as enigmatic as life itself.

Shakespeare the Dramatist

In his portrayal of the character of Iago Shakespeare has made an invaluable contribution to the characterisation of the villainy that men can descend to. Iago's villainy is for the sake of villainy, almost as if he is evil personified. Still, judged by conventional standards, he has his strong points: he is not a drunkard; he is not a philanderer; and he is a man of iron self-control.

Owing to his intended, and finally accomplished villainy towards his fellowmen, our hearts cannot warm to him. The ordinary sinful man who, because of the warmth of his heart, succumbs to the vice of the flesh, can win our sympathy. But not Iago. He is never relaxed but at all times like a serpent approaching the very heart of his victims, unobserved. With all these thoughts in mind, now read the speech aloud but, like the serpent, slowly.

Speech 2: "That Cassio loves her, I do well believe 't"

IAGO

> That Cassio loves her, I do well believe 't;
> That she loves him, 'tis apt and of great credit.
> The Moor, howbeit that I endure him not,
> Is of a constant, loving, noble nature,
> And I dare think he'll prove to Desdemona   5
> A most dear husband. Now I do love her too;
> Not out of absolute lust, though peradventure
> I stand accountant for as great a sin,
> But partly led to diet my revenge,
> For that I do suspect the lusty Moor   10
> Hath leaped into my seat; the thought whereof
> Doth, like a poisonous mineral, gnaw my inwards;
> And nothing can or shall content my soul
> Till I am evened with him, wife for wife;
> Or failing so, yet that I put the Moor   15
> At least into a jealousy so strong
> That judgement cannot cure. Which thing to do,
> If this poor trash of Venice, whom I trash
> For his quick hunting, stand the putting on,
> I'll have our Michael Cassio on the hip,   20
> Abuse him to the Moor in the rank garb
> (For I fear Cassio with my nightcap too),
> Make the Moor thank me, love me, and reward me
> For making him egregiously an ass
> And practising upon his peace and quiet   25
> Even to madness. 'Tis here, but yet confused:
> Knavery's plain face is never seen till used.

2   **'tis apt and of great credit:**
         it is most likely and credible

3   **howbeit that I endure him not:**
     although I cannot tolerate him

5-6   **he'll prove to Desdemona/A most dear husband:**
      he will be loved by Desdemona and be a loving
      husband to her

7-8   **peradventure/I stand accountant for as great a sin:**
      perhaps I am accountable for so great a sin

9   **partly led to diet my revenge:**
     (I am) behaving in this way to feed my revenge

10-11 **the lusty Moor/Hath leaped into my seat:**
       the lustful Moor has slept with my wife

14   **Till I am evened with him:** till I get even with him

18   **whom I trash:** whom I check (keep in control)

20   **I'll have our Michael Cassio on the hip:**
     I will have Cassio at my mercy

21   **Abuse him to the Moor in the rank garb:**
     slander Cassio to the Moor in a gross manner

22   **I fear Cassio with my nightcap too:**
     I suspect Cassio of having been in bed with my wife too

Speech 3

"Think'st thou I'ld make a life of jealousy"

A Technical Achievement

Act III scene iii in *Othello* is one of the greatest scenes in all literature. It is a technical achievement of the highest order and has no match in any other Shakespearean play. But the scene must be read in full, read and re-read, with sufficient time and thought to ponder over each and every line.

It is a scene in which we witness the diabolic cunning of Iago as he begins to cast his mesmerising spell over the open mind of Othello, his main victim. Here we see him injecting his first shot of poison into Othello's mind and then when the time is ripe, sow seeds of doubt and disquiet which eventually destroy the man. Every word and every gesture in this fast-paced scene draws the play to its climax and with every word and gesture, Iago moves like a deadly insect, stalking and stinging his victim to death. And each move is perfectly timed by him. It ends with the beginning of the moral decline of the main character of the play, who, as a result of Iago's poison of jealousy, changes from a husband with the fondest love and unbounded confidence for his wife Desdemona, to a man tortured by jealousy and the madness of hatred of her.

A Husband and Wife Scene

As we read scene iii (in its entirety), we can find it horrifying.

(a) To watch a sinister Iago at work, purposely poisoning the mind of a husband against his faithful and loving wife can be distressing.

(b) To listen to his devious intellect and his "witchcraft" can make us feel ill at ease.

Yet, for a short spell, we have the lovely scene of Othello and Desdemona:

(a) We hear them expressing their love for each other.

(b) We look at the young wife who looks upon herself as an equal partner in marriage.

(c) We hear her, because of her love for Othello, pleading for the reconciliation between him and Cassio, his second-in-Command.

(d) As the wife of Othello she feels she has the right to do so.

It is a beautiful little scene in itself , standing in strong contrast to the rest of Act III scene iii and ending with a complete affirmation of Othello's love for Desdemona. But even here there is the hint of the terrible loss he is about to experience, the loss of love and the loss of faith in her love. There is a dramatic foreshadowing of future events when Othello tells Desdemona:

> "Perdition catch my soul
> But I do love thee and when I love thee not
> Chaos is come again."

Standing near at hand is one Iago, ready to pounce with his sting of poison. The poison will later on work, Othello will turn against the wife he loves so dearly and chaos will have its bloody reign.

The Poisoning of Othello's Mind

If you have the opportunity to read the scene in full, before coming to the speech of Othello in this chapter, you will notice how it grows in intensity, portraying the psychological changes wrought in the mind of a noble character by a devilish Iago. It is a scene of inner action:

(a) Illustrating how suspicion can be created by insinuation and left to feed and grow upon itself.

(b) The suspicion is fostered by the use of undefined insinuations against Desdemona's fidelity.

(c) It requires great skill to avoid explicit accusations against her, because Iago knows that Othello is still deeply in love with his wife.

(d) Therefore every word, every idea, must be skilfully manipulated if the poison is to go to the mind and the heart of Othello.

Various Stages in the Baiting

It is important to note the various stages in the baiting of Othello: they help us to see the mind of Iago at work:

(a) The baiting of Othello begins with a single statement from him: "Ha! I like not that." He has seen Desdemona and Cassio in quiet conversation together and Iago makes sure that Othello has seen it too.

(b) Othello innocently asks what Iago does not like.

(c) Iago feigns confusion and then lapses into silence - to give Othello's mind time to wonder.

(d) Iago asks a question that is seemingly innocent : "Did Michael Cassio, when you woo'd my lady, know of your loves?"

(e) It is not so innocent. There is an insinuation in that question which stirs Othello's curiosity.

(f) Iago, always alert, is aware of Othello's curiosity. He decides to excite this curiosity by simply repeating Othello's own words each time, almost like a parrot. He adds to the excitement with half-expressed thoughts about Cassio's honesty, which intensifies the doubt in his victim's mind.

(g) Iago watches Othello and sees the effect of his veiled insinuations. He is pleased with the progress of his plan so far and decides to be more explicit, but first of all with a visual sign of his own doubt about Cassio:

— he purses his brow as an indication of his own worry.

— he excites Othello's curiosity by timing his answers.

— he forces Othello to make him reveal his thoughts about Cassio.

(h) Iago knows he has planted the seed of suspicion with his sly suggestion of a disbelief in Cassio's honesty.

(i) He knows too that he has still to be careful. He delays giving concrete evidence about this. He:

— pretends to be uncertain about it.

— alludes to his own natural tendency to spy into abuses.

— cautions Othello about the danger of prying.

— warns Othello "O beware, my lord, of jealousy".

(j) The effect on Othello of Iago's poison is obvious: his curiosity has become suspicion and now there is a hint of jealousy itself, the green-eyed monster that destroys the innocent and the guilty. But Othello is half aware of the effect on himself. He tries to shake himself out of this hypnotic effect and makes a dignified rejection of all of Iago's insinuations: "Think'st thou I'ld make a life of jealousy?" he asks Iago. Yet, what he is really doing is asking himself and probing into his own mind about the fidelity of his own wife.

(k) The poison injected by Iago is working. He knows he is beginning to have doubts and that he is not a man to suffer the agony of doubts of his wife: "to be once in doubt, is once to be resolv'd."

(l) He fights hard with himself and examines the qualities of Desdemona, searching for confirmation of her faithfulness:

— he knows she is fair, loves company, is free of speech.

— she sings, plays and dances.

— he tries to assure himself that these are all virtues.

(m) He examines his own weak points and convinces himself that there is no need to fear or doubt: "She had eyes and chose me."

(n) But he knows the doubt is there and tries to put it aside: "I'll see before I doubt, when I doubt, prove." The seeds of the possibility of Desdemona's unfaithfulness have been planted in his subconscious mind.

(o) Iago has been watching the agitated Othello all the time and he is becoming more confident and is able to speak with "franker spirit". Up to this point he has been insinuating in general terms about Cassio and Desdemona. Now he links them together and advises Othello: "Look to your wife, observe her well with Cassio."

(p) With cunning he puts on a mask of loyal concern and apologises for imparting this suspicion on Desdemona but he knows Othello is in his power.

(q) Yet he has to be careful. He pounces on the thought of the fickleness of women in general, then comes to emphasise particular aspects:

— the adultery of Venetian women.

— the fact that Desdemona has in the past refused many suitors.

— the fact that in marrying him she had deceived her father.

(r) We can picture the chaos in Othello's mind. He thinks his wife is honest and thinks that she is not. He gives vent to the feelings of grief that are building up in his mind and utters a groan of agony: "why did I marry?"

In this groan we have come to the climax of the scene. It is the highest point of tension and the turning point in the play. Iago's poison has conjured up in the mind of Othello a hideous, powerful thought - a monstrous image of Desdemona's infidelity. What adds to the tragedy is the fact that it has all been concocted by a villain, and that a noble character is now possessed by a devil and has fallen into his trap. The noble character may try to put the horrible thought aside: "away at once with love or jealousy", but we know how jealousy will soon eat into his soul and what the end will be.

Speech 3: "Think'st thou I'ld make a life of jealousy"

OTHELLO

     Think'st thou I'ld make a life of jealousy,
To follow still the changes of the moon
With fresh suspicions? No! To be once in doubt
Is once to be resolved. Exchange me for a goat
When I shall turn the business of my soul   5
To such exsufflicate and blown surmises,
Matching this inference. 'Tis not to make me jealous
To say my wife is fair, feeds well, loves company,
Is free of speech, sings, plays, and dances;
Where virtue is, these are more virtuous.   10
Nor from mine own weak merits will I draw
The smallest fear or doubt of her revolt,
For she had eyes, and chose me. No, Iago;
I'll see before I doubt; when I doubt, prove;
And on the proof there is no more but this -   15
Away at once with love or jealousy!

3-4 **To be once in doubt/Is once to be resolved:**
    to have the least doubt is to be totally convinced

6 **To such exsufflicate and blown surmises:**
    to such exaggerated and ill-founded suspicions

7 **'Tis not to make me jealous:**
    it is not sufficient to make me jealous

11-12 **Nor from my own weak merits will I draw/The smallest fear:**
    just because I do not deserve her love is no reason for me to fear (that she is unfaithful)

Speech 4

"This fellow's of exceeding honesty"

Iago's poison at work

After the "baiting" episode with Iago, we see Othello rushing to his doom with accelerating speed. Jealousy has begun to take control of him, a devastating control, driving out all love for Desdemona and we see this great man writhing under the torment of suspecting what he had once loved. His was a trusting nature, not easily given to jealousy, but now poisoned by the insinuations of the stings of Iago, he is "perplex'd in the extreme".

He is undergoing a horrible mental torture and anguish of the keenest woe, suffering:

(a)   conflict between love and hate.

(b)   conflict between tenderness and resentment.

(c)   conflict between jealousy and remorse.

Our Involvement in His Agony

Othello was a man who had achieved so much in military affairs. He was essentially noble. He was a man of outstanding virtues with the grand simplicity of the barbarian in his love of his wife and the rapture of chivalry and fond protectiveness for her. But one flaw in his nature destroyed him: it was not just personal pride; it was the anguish of despair for human purity and truth; it was jealousy, and he allowed himself to be debased by the passion of jealousy which humiliates and destroys all.

In all of our own natures there is at least a little of the same kind of impulses that agitated such a noble character as Othello. His punishment and his downfall fill us with emotions of pity and fear, fear that if a man of such excellent qualities can receive such a blow in life, what can we expect of life? Our involvement generates sympathy for the hero of the play and results in a deeper understanding of him.

Nature of the Moor

(a)   He is noble, confiding, tender and generous.

(b)   But his blood is of a most inflammable kind.

(c)   Once roused by the sense of wrongs, real or imagined, his revenge is stopped by no consideration of remorse or pity; it can only find relief in the dictates of rage and despair.

(d)   His jealousy controls the mind, never quitting, growing stronger and stronger at every moment of delay, until it becomes a tide of deep, sustained passion, impetuous but majestic.

Jealousy Destroys Othello

As we come to the fourth speech of this selection we can see the effects of the poison of jealousy on the mind of Othello:

(a)   Already it is destroying him.

(b)   His capacity for judging clearly is deteriorating: he cannot see through the wiles of Iago and looks upon him as a fellow "of exceeding honesty" with a sound knowledge of "human dealings".

(c)   He has lost the desire for concrete proof of Desdemona's guilt and is prepared to accept less in the way of solid evidence: a misplaced handkerchief or a fictitious dream.

(d)   He has lost confidence in himself. He sees the problem of the "colour bar" in his marriage to a white woman: "I am black". He see the problem of the "age barrier" between himself and his wife: "I am declin'd into the vale of years". And the problem of his lack of "those soft parts of conversation that chamberers have".

(e) He is accepting, without proof, Desdemona's infidelity as an accomplished fact: "She's gone; I am abused".

(f) He is prepared to condemn all married women: marriage for him is now a "curse", calling "delicate creatures ours" but having no control over "their appetites" for love.

(g) He sees relief for his mental torture in hatred and loathing: "my relief must be to loathe her".

(h) His faith in human nature turns to one of pessimism: we are all, he says, great men and base alike, fated to be deceived even from the time of our birth - it is our "plague", our "destiny", as inevitable as death itself.

Pathetic Picture

This picture of Othello under the power of jealousy pulls at the heart strings:

(a) He was once the leader of men and the deliverer of Cyprus.

(b) Now he sees himself as black, old, and without the gifts of love-talk.

(c) Soon we will hear him bid farewell to some of the things he loved most in life:

— the pride, the pomp, the circumstance of glorious war.

— the tranquil mind, happiness, neighing steeds.

— the sound of trumpets, drums, and fifes.

His farewell will fall upon our ears like drum-beats of doom, and make us realise that he has lost all control and wants only black vengeance and tyrannous hate. We know that it is a distraught Othello that calls aloud "I'll tear her all to pieces". And we know the villain who caused this.

Speech 4: "This fellow's of exceeding honesty"

OTHELLO

> This fellow's of exceeding honesty,
> And knows all qualities, with a learned spirit
> Of human dealings. If I do prove her haggard,
> Though that her jesses were my dear heartstrings,
> I'd whistle her off and let her down the wind   5
> To prey at fortune. Haply, for I am black
> And have not those soft parts of conversation
> That chamberers have, or for I am declined
> Into the vale of years - yet that's not much -
> She's gone. I am abused, and my relief   10
> Must be to loathe her. O curse marriage,
> That we can call these delicate creatures ours,
> And not their appetites! I had rather be a toad
> And live upon the vapour of a dungeon
> Than keep a corner in the thing I love   15
> For others' uses. Yet 'tis the plague of great ones;
> Prerogatived are they less than the base.
> 'Tis destiny unshunnable, like death.
> Even then this forked plague is fated to us
> When we do quicken.   20

2   **knows all qualities, with a learned spirit:**
     with his experience he is able to understand all types of
     people perceptively

3   **If I do prove her haggard:**
     if I prove her unfaithful in her behaviour

4   **Though that her jesses were my dear heartstrings:**
     even if she is attached to my heart like a hawk with
     leather thongs attached to its feet

5   **I'd whistle her off:** I would get rid of her

5-6   **let her down the wind/To prey at fortune:**
> let her make her own way in the world (i.e., divorce her)

7-8   **have not those soft parts ... chamberers have:**
> have not the talents for conversation that ladies' men
> have

10   **I am abused:** I have been deceived

17   **Prerogatived are they less than the base:**
> rich people are less likely than the poor to be deceived
> in marriage

19-20   **this forked plague is fated to us/When we do quicken:**
> we are fated to be deceived (by our wives) when we are
> born

Speech 5

"It is the cause, it is the cause, my soul"

Picture of Desdemona before Her Murder

Iago's poison of jealousy has taken possession of Othello and soon we see him descending to the catastrophe of the murder of his wife. The time is ripe therefore to have a final look at the wife who is about to be murdered:

(a) Throughout the play she shows herself to be a lady of beauty, wit and duty.

(b) We remember how with greedy ear she devoured Othello's tales of battles, sieges and disastrous moving accidents on the open seas.

(c) We recall how she loved him for the dangers he had experienced, and how he loved her because she pitied him.

(d) We know that basically their marriage was one of intellect and spiritual compatibility.

(e) · She was of noble lineage, the daughter of a distinguished member of the Venetian oligarchy, but out of love abandoned her family to become the wife of Othello.

(f) In a previous scene we witnessed Othello striking her and in a passion of rage ordering her out of his sight. It was an intensely powerful scene emphasising the pathetic, submissive helplessness of this lovely wife.

(g) We heard no word of recrimination from her. Out of loyalty to him she accepted his anger, as a dumb animal would.

(h) She accepted his anger, not blaming him, but looking for a cause in herself.

(i)   We know she is not the cause. It is the jealousy devouring the soul of her husband.

A Look at the Murderer

The enormity of the murder of Desdemona is heightened by several facts:

(a)   She is completely innocent of all accusations of infidelity.

(b)   It is a murder committed by her own loved and loving husband.

(c)   It is not a murder committed on the spur of the moment nor in the heat of passion.

(d)   It is premeditated, with Othello having had plenty of time between his decision to "tear her all to pieces" and the actual killing itself.

The man guilty of such an enormous crime therefore merits a closer look in an attempt to discover the "why" and the "wherefore" of his action:

(a)   He is no ordinary man, but a man of dignity and nobility.

(b)   His tragedy is not just an ordinary squalid story of crime, of murder for the sake of murder.

(c)   It is a murder caused by jealousy in the mind and heart of a leader of men who has the torrid passions of the South.

(d)   He is a man of physical courage and charm, normally free from all pettiness. But he has one defect in his character: he is too self-centred

(e)   In such a man, once jealousy is aroused, he dwells too long on his own lost pride to the exclusion of all other considerations. He does not give sufficient time or thought to the possibility of his wife's innocence.

(f) This defect plunges him into the wrong conclusions about the truth, and becomes an uncontrollable driving force within himself towards catastrophe for himself and others.

(g) He had the opportunity of the freedom of a choice: to believe in his wife's innocence or not to believe. But confrontation with a choice demands careful thought and investigation. Othello is not made for thought. He is a man who acts on impulse and instinct. That, at times, brings about disaster and therein lies the tragedy of Othello: choice for him is impossible.

A Scene before the Murder of Desdemona

In Act V scene i, the dramatist focuses our minds on events prior to the murder of Desdemona, as a preparation for it and makes it more effective by its very contrast:

(a) The scene takes place in the open streets at night.

(b) Roderigo, following Iago's advice, waits to engage in a struggle with Cassio.

(c) We hear the rasp of steel upon steel, the cries and shouts of the onlookers, the sound of the quick hurrying of feet.

(d) In the struggle Roderigo wounds Cassio.

(e) Iago, to protect himself, kills Roderigo.

(f) It is a scene of darkness, ambush and murder, and out of all the confusion comes the undoing of Iago.

The Murder of Desdemona

We have now arrived at the terrifying moment we have been waiting for ever since we saw the effect of Iago's poison on Othello's mind. It is now a different atmosphere:

(a) We leave the dark, noisy streets and enter a scene of peace, a bedchamber in Othello's castle, with Desdemona asleep. A light burns beside her bed.

(b) There is no sound, no outward sign of the horror that is about to fall on the scene.

(c) There is no movement, except the flickering of the bedside light.

(d) The door of the bedchamber opens noiselessly and the draught makes the flame of the light leap up.

(e) We see the wide-staring eyes of Othello, the murderer, and have time to study the man:

— he is obviously in sorrow, boundless sorrow.

— he is serene, with some of the signs of his normal composure and self-control.

— he approaches his wife's bed stealthily and whispers to himself: "It is the cause, it is the cause, my soul".

— we can see at once that he is determined to kill her and if we look carefully into his mind at this moment we have the feeling that he has come to this decision after a careful evaluation of the evidence: but we know that his evaluation is wrong.

— he has all the appearance of a man approaching the task of killing, as a priest about to perform a ritual sacrifice.

— he looks down at his beautiful wife, at peace in her sleep and he falters, yet proud of his own cool command: "I'll not shed her blood".

— he is convinced of the necessity of killing. In his eyes it is not a crime, but a necessity, a calculated sacrifice to justice: "It is the cause, it is the cause".

— he has already convinced himself of the reason for this: "she must die, else she'll betray more men".

— he glances at the burning bedside taper and cannot bear the light: "Put out the light", he whispers.

— he glances at Desdemona and is convulsed with the thought of what he is about to do: "once put out thy light".

— she, he knows, is the "pattern of excelling nature" and we realise he is still in love with her and we experience some of his intense emotion.

— Othello is a man not at peace with himself. He is torn between a powerful love for his wife and a terrible conviction that she must be punished by him.

— he searches for justification of his decision to be judge, jury, and executioner of his wife so that what he is about to do will not be a crime of passion or an act of revenge. In his own way he finds this justification: "I'll kill thee/ And love thee after".

— he has always been a man of clear decisions and decides even now that this horrible deed must be done. But love again takes over and he feels that it would be an act of generosity on his part to allow her time to acknowledge her guilt and prepare her soul: "I would not kill thy unprepared spirit,/I would not kill thy soul".

— before the deed, he gives her a kiss and Desdemona wakens. When she knows "the cause" she makes a heartfelt plea to allow her to call Cassio as witness of her innocence.

— the very sound of the name Cassio makes Othello lose control. His eyes roll, he gnaws his nether lip and bloody passion shakes his manly frame.

— he attempts to smother her, looks at her again and realises she is not yet dead. He accepts the fact that what he is doing is "cruel" but "merciful" and so that she will not linger in her pain, he smothers her to death.

— in the final smothering we hear the rustling of the bed clothes, the heavy breathing of Othello and the final short gasp of Desdemona.

— the murder has been committed in a scene of pity and horror. An innocent life has met disaster which has gone beyond all recovery.

After the Murder

The crime itself shocks us, as we know it is a crime against an innocent person. But what shocks us all the more are the cruel accusations of Othello against his wife after murdering her: "She was a whore./She's like a liar gone to burning hell!" Our first reaction to Desdemona's murder and Othello's horrible accusations against his loving wife is one of condemnation, but as we sit back and look at the full picture of Othello we can still find some pity for him:

(a)   He is an extrovert, a man suited for action and not perception, reflection or understanding.

(b)   He is a man who feels self-justified, not acting out of hatred: "Naught did I in hate, but all in honour".

(c)   He is a man whose action becomes the instrument of his own cruxificion.

(d)   When he learns the truth of his wife's innocence, the sight of such beauty destroyed by his jealousy becomes a harrowing sight for him: "This look of thine will hurl my soul from heaven/And fiends will snatch at it".

(e)   He is prepared to accept the punishment for his crime and we hear him cry: "Whip me, you devils/From the possession of this heavenly sight/Blow me about in winds, roast me in sulphur,/Wash me in steep down gulfs of liquid-fire".

(f)   Finally, the sight of this murderer, giving his farewell kiss to the corpse of the wife he loved, is heart-rending:

— it gives us the feeling that he and Desdemona are now reconciled in that kiss.

— it suggests the possibility of his own religious redemption.

When we see him thrusting the knife into his own body and dying, we can only accuse him of being foolish and overtrusting. We may hate him but we do not despise him. He is now as always was, a man more to be pitied for loving "not wisely" but "too well".

Speech 5: "It is the cause, it is the cause, my soul"

Desdemona [asleep] in her bed. Enter Othello with a light.

OTHELLO

           It is the cause, it is the cause, my soul.
Let me not name it to you, you chaste stars!
It is the cause. Yet I'll not shed her blood,
Nor scar that whiter skin of hers than snow,
And smooth as monumental alabaster.   5
Yet she must die, else she'll betray more men.
Put out the light, and then put out the light.
If I quench thee, thou flaming minister,
I can again thy former light restore,
Should I repent me; but once put out thy light,   10
Thou cunning'st pattern of excelling nature,
I know not where is that Promethean heat
That can thy light relume. When I have plucked the rose,
I cannot give it vital growth again;
It needs must wither. I'll smell thee on the tree.   15
    [He kisses her.]
O balmy breath, that dost almost persuade
Justice to break her sword! One more, one more!
Be thus when thou art dead, and I will kill thee,
And love thee after. One more, and that's the last!
So sweet was ne'er so fatal. I must weep,   20
But they are cruel tears. This sorrow's heavenly;
It strikes where it doth love. She wakes.

1   **It is the cause:** it is the offence, the reason

4   **scar that whiter skin of hers than snow:**
    blemish Desdemona's skin which is whiter than snow

7   **Put out the light, and then put out the light:**
    extinguish the lit taper and then strangle Desdemona

8   **thou flaming minister:** the lit taper

11   **Thou cunning'st pattern of excelling nature:**
     you most exquisite work of nature

12   **Promethean heat:**
     Prometheus stole fire from the gods and was punished with
     everlasting fire

13   **That can thy light relume:**
     that can rekindle your light, bring you back to life

16   **balmy breath:** breath that soothes

20   **So sweet was ne'er so fatal:**
     nothing so sweet was ever so deadly (as this last kiss)

Questions

1.   "Othello is one of the great lovers in the literature of the
     world; for him Desdemona is the whole meaning of life." Is
     this statement completely true? How can such a lover descend
     to the degrading depths of sexual jealousy? What brings about
     this degradation?

2.   "Othello's credulity borders upon stupidity and this is not a
     quality acceptable in a tragic hero; the play, therefore, suffers
     from this central flaw." Do you accept this viewpoint?

3.   "Iago dominates the play because he possesses exceptional
     qualities of will and intellect." Do you agree?

Memorable Lines

I, i: "Preferment goes by letter and affection,
            And not by old gradation."

"We cannot all be masters, nor all masters
Cannot be truly followed."

"In following him, I follow but myself;
Heaven is my judge, not I for love and duty,
But seeming so, for my peculiar end."

"I will wear my heart upon my sleeve
For daws to peck at; I am not what I am."

I, ii: "I fetch my life and being
From men of royal siege."

                    "You shall more command with years
Than with your weapons."

"So opposite to marriage that she shunned
The wealthy curled darlings of our nation."

I, iii: "A maiden never bold;
Of spirit so still and quiet that her motion
Blushed at herself."

"She'd come again, and with a greedy ear
Devour up my discourse."

"She gave me for my pains a world of sighs.
....
And I loved her that she did pity them."

"When remedies are past, the griefs are ended
By seeing the worst, which late on hopes depended."

"He robs himself that spends a bootless grief."

"I saw Othello's visage in his mind."

"Look to her, Moor, if thou hast eyes to see:
She has deceived her father, and may thee."

II, i: "She puts her tongue a little in her heart
And chides with thinking."

"You are pictures out of doors,
Bells in your parlors, wildcats in your kitchens,
Saints in your injuries, devils being offended,
Players in your housewifery, and housewives in your
beds.

"If it were now to die,
'Twere now to be most happy."

II, iii: "Reputation is an idle and most false imposition; oft got
without merit and lost without deserving."

"I'll pour this pestilence into his ear,
That she repeals him for her body's lust."

III, i: "Thereby hangs a tale."

III, iii: "Excellent wretch! Perdition catch my soul
But I do love thee! And when I love thee not,
Chaos is come again."

"Men should be what they seem."

"Good name in man and woman, dear my lord,
Is the immediate jewel of their souls.
Who steals my purse, steals trash; 'tis something, nothing;
'Twas mine, 'tis his, and has been slave to thousands;
But he that filches from me my good name
Robs me of that which not enriches him
And makes me poor indeed."

"O, beware, my lord, of jealousy!
It is the green-eyed monster, which doth mock
The meat it feeds on."

"O curse marriage,
That we call these delicate creatures ours,
And not their appetites!"

"Arise, black vengeance, from the hollow hell!"

"My bloody thoughts, with violent pace,
Shall ne'er look back, ne'er ebb to humble love,
Till that a capable and wide revenge
Swallow them up."

III, iv: "'Tis not a year or two shows us a man.
They are all but stomachs, and we all but food;
They eat us hungerly, and when they are full,
They belch us."

IV, ii: "I will be hanged if some eternal villain,
Some busy and insinuating rogue,
Some cogging, cozening slave, to get some office,
Have not devised this slander."

"His unkindness may defeat my life,
But never taint my love."

IV, iii: "I do think it is their husbands' faults
If wives do fall."

"Let husbands know
Their wives have sense like them. They see, and smell,
And have their palates both for sweet and sour,
As husbands have. What is it that they do
When they change us for others? Is it sport?
I think it is. And doth affection breed it?
I think it doth. Is 't frailty that thus errs?
It is so too. And have not we affections?
Desires for sport? And frailty? As men have?
Then let them use us well; else let them know,
The ills we do, their ills instruct us so."

V, ii: "If you bethink yourself of any crime
Unreconciled as yet to heaven and grace,
Solicit for it straight."

V, ii: "You're fatal then
When your eyes roll so.

"That death's unnatural that kills for loving."

        "May his pernicious soul
Rot half a grain a day."

"This look of thine will hurl my soul from heaven,
And fiends will snatch at it."

        "Whip me, ye devils,
From the possession of this heavenly sight!
Blow me about in winds! roast me in sulphur!
Wash me in steep-down gulfs of liquid fire."

"Naught did I in hate, but all in honour."

"Speak of me as I am. Nothing extenuate,
Nor set down aught in malice. Then you speak
Of one that loved not wisely, but too well;
Of one not easily jealous, but, being wrought,
Perplexed in the extreme; of one whose hand,
Like the base Judean, threw a pearl away
Richer than all his tribe."

"Come not between the dragon and his wrath."

photograph on page 79
shows Eric Porter
as King Lear

A Glance at

KING LEAR

Date of the Play

The play was written about 1605-1606. It belongs to the same period as *Hamlet*, *Othello* and *Macbeth*.

Play in Outline

King Lear wishes to retire as ruler of his country and decides to divide his kingdom equally among his three daughters but his gift is dependent upon a public declaration of their love for him. Goneril and Regan are fulsome in their protestations of love for their father but they are really serpents, tigers at heart. Cordelia, the youngest, is of a gentler nature and utters only a simple expression of duty and affection for him. Lear is enraged at her apparent coolness and disowns her. He does not see through the hollowness of her sisters' pretensions and divides his kingdom between the two of them.

In a similar fashion the Earl of Gloucester wrongs a dutiful son, Edgar, his legitimate child, and raises an undeserving son Edmund, to power. He is deceived by the apparent sincerity of the crafty Edmund.

All the disasters follow the actions of the two fathers. Goneril, Lear's eldest daughter, as soon as she obtains control, treats her father with disrespect and at once reduces his retinue of followers. He leaves the castle and goes off, hoping to find happiness at his daughter Regan's home.

Regan refuses to allow her father into her home until he apologises to Goneril, and Lear now is aware that they are both in league against him. In anger he sets out into a wild night in the company of his faithful bitter Fool who loses no opportunity in reminding his master of the folly of giving away his kingdom.

Edmund convinces his father Gloucester that Edgar is a villain. Both fathers are now open to further misfortunes.

Lear has wandered on to a stormy heath and sought refuge in a hovel occupied by Edgar in disguise as poor mad Tom O'Bedlam. Gloucester comes to the hovel, sees Lear in an unbalanced state of mind and persuades him to find shelter in a farmhouse. They hear of the plot of Goneril and Regan against Gloucester's son. Edmund has also been plotting against his father's life by producing evidence of an imminent invasion of the country by the French and untruthfully suggesting that Gloucester has played a part in the plan.

Gloucester is blinded and insists on going to the cliffs of Dover to end his life there. Edgar acts as his father's guide and contrives a ruse by which the old man thinks he has fallen from the cliffs but has miraculously escaped death.

Things begin to happen very quickly. The French army arrives in Britain and Cordelia finds her father dressed with flowers. She cares for him tenderly. He believes he has been miraculously snatched from death. Albany, Goneril's "mild husband", denounces her for her cruelty. Goneril and Regan add lust for Edmund to their crimes. Edmund becomes commander-in-chief of the English forces.

The French forces are defeated. Lear and Cordelia become Edmund's prisoners. Edmund issues a secret order for the execution. Goneril, because of her jealousy, poisons Regan, and then stabs herself. Gloucester dies of a broken heart. Albany arrests Edmund on a charge of capital treason. In a formal combat Edgar gives Edmund a mortal wound. Lear and Cordelia have a happy reunion in prison but it is short-lived. Cordelia is hanged and Lear dies of a broken heart. Edgar and Albany are left to restore the kingdom.

Theme of the Play

Shakespeare's greatest tragedies, *Macbeth*, *Othello*, *King Lear*, and *Hamlet* have all one underlying common theme: they are all concerned with some tragic flaw in the main character:

(a) Macbeth of overreaching ambition.

(b) Othello of cankerous jealousy.

(c) Lear of lack of insight as father and king.

(d) Hamlet of too scrupulous a conscience.

In them we see men at odds with the moral order of things as this was understood in Shakespeare's time.

Disruption of the Natural Order

Lear disturbs this natural order. He is a king and he abdicates: he surrenders his position, his power and authority to his daughters and, in doing so, brings dire consequences not only on himself but on the very daughters whom he wishes to benefit.

This is the main theme of *King Lear*: man's misuse of the delegated authority of God which brings about disasters of varying magnitude on himself and the world at large. In addition to this, the play has two other themes:

(a) of parent-child relationship.

(b) of redemption through suffering.

Parent-Child Relationship

The parent has a double role to fulfil. He is, first of all, protector and guardian, a provider of food, clothing and shelter for the child which the child reciprocates with love and gratitude. At the same time, he has another important function: for the child's own good he must guide, direct and at times steer the child away from what is not healthy for him or her.

Admittedly this is a most heavy responsibility. It requires the utmost tact and sympathetic understanding on the part of the parent. Without these, the parent can so easily appear as a tyrant in the eyes of his own son or daughter and can so easily arouse rebellious feelings and even hatred.

This theme is well developed in the play: Lear genuinely loves his daughters but he lacks tact in his dealings with them. His self-centredness arouses the mutiny and hatred of his two elder daughters. The theme is echoed in the sub-plot (Gloucester has two sons: one loves him and the other plots against his life).

Redemption through Suffering

Lear suffers cruelly at the hands of his two elder daughters, Regan and Goneril. He is partly responsible for his own suffering: there are aspects of his character that merit their disapproval. He is arrogant and dictatorial. Through suffering he becomes a better and more human (and therefore more lovable) a person - his suffering has taught him his own shortcomings as a king and he bitterly regrets his neglect of his poorer subjects.

Gloucester, too, has suffered horribly by being blinded. But his new way of life has also made others suffer, particularly one of his sons, Edgar. He now sees truth more clearly and wins the love of Edgar, the son he has wronged.

Both Themes

The two themes deal with violated filial ties, hatred, deceit and egotism, but the total effect is not one of pessimism. As the play ends we are left with the impression that the future looks good: the end is victory through redemption, not defeat.

Selection of Memorable Speeches

(1)   "Thou, nature, art my goddess."
             Act I, scene ii, lines 1-22.   (Edmund)

(2)   "Hear, nature hear; dear goddess hear."
             Act I, scene iv, lines 262-278.   (Lear)

(3)   "I am ashamed that thou hast power to shake my
             manhood thus."
             Act I, scene iv, lines 283-297.   (Lear)

(4) & (5)   "Blow, winds, and crack your cheeks! rage blow!"
             "Rumble thy bellyful! spit, spout, rain."
             Act III, scene ii, lines 1-24.   (Lear)

(6)   "Hold your hands in benediction o'er me."
             Act IV, scene vii, lines 48-85.   (Cordelia, Lear)

Speech 1

"Thou, nature, art my goddess"

Introduction

In Act I scene i the main theme of the play is introduced: Lear abdicates and hands over all his authority to his two daughters, Goneril and Regan. They plan at once to rid him of all power and position.

In Act I scene ii the same theme is repeated: Edmund, the illegitimate, aspires to the position which is the rightful inheritance of Edgar, the natural born son of the Earl of Gloucester. To achieve this he plans to betray his father and his brother.

The Gloucester-story adds emphasis to the Lear-story and demonstrates that the sins that the dramatist is attacking are common to all levels of society, king and subject. King Lear and his subject, the Earl of Gloucester, have both disinherited natural heirs and bring misery to themselves and their families. Both plots in the play run on parallel lines and it is most interesting to watch how they develop and at times intertwine.

Character of the Speaker

Society has punished Edmund for his illegitimacy by depriving him of his inheritance. His natural pride in his person and talents is stung when he hears his father speak of the circumstances of his birth. He naturally feels sorely aggrieved and is stirred to envy, hatred and a lust for power. In his own mind he feels entitled to take revenge not only on society but on his father and his brother Edgar who are stumbling blocks to achieving his goal.

The shame of his birth has generated in him a sense of guilt which has sharpened in his heart a predisposition to evil. His evil intentions and actions are mostly directed towards his father and his brother. We can sympathise with him in his defence of his rights as a son of Gloucester, but where he errs is, in order to achieve this right, this power, he is prepared to take away the rights of his brother Edgar. There is no justice in such an attitude. His speech may appeal to the modern man or woman for in it he states the rights of those who are illegitimate (the bastards of our society) but we can hardly sympathise with him when we see the means he uses to achieve these rights. Let us take a closer look at this victim of society:

(a) He refuses to abide by the "plague of custom" which deprives illegitimates from a share of an inheritance.

(b) He refuses to accept that simply because he is younger than Edgar, he has no entitlement: he looks upon this idea of society as "outdated".

(c) He is aware of his own talents:

— he has the strength and beauty of early manhood.

— he is endowed with a powerful intellect.

— he has charm of personality which he can use for his own ends.

— he has the ability to understand the strengths and weaknesses of his associates.

— he is a man of strong energetic will with an enormous lust for power which allows no one to stand in his way, not even a father nor a brother.

(d) He is prepared to ridicule society and the "foppery of the world", the men who throw the blame for human folly and crimes on the influence of the stars.

(e) He leaves us in no doubt as to his methods in his rise to power:

> Legitimate Edgar, I must have your land:
>
> ....
>
> Well, my legitimate, if this letter speed,
> And my invention thrive, Edmund the base
> Shall top the legitimate.

And these methods of achieving power are the methods of an immoral and a treacherous man:

— they require the betrayal of a credulous, suspicious father

— they demand the forging of a letter in order to supplant a brother who is the natural heir to the earldom.

But all this does not worry Edmund in the least. He is even proud of his villainy and acknowledges it. He is proud of the fact that "the base" shall top "the legitimate".

Edmund is the villain of the play but Shakespeare has prevented his villainy from slipping into monstrosity by endowing him with many talents. He has the charm to win the love of many around him - his father, Goneril and Regan, but he abuses this charm. He is brought to a deserving end, slain by the brother he has wronged, but even then his fate is nobly tragic: his wheel has come full circle.

Speech 1: "Thou, nature, art my goddess"

EDMUND

>   Thou nature, art my goddess; to thy law
> My services are bound. Wherefore should I
> Stand in the plague of custom, and permit
> The curiosity of nations to deprive me,
> For that I am some twelve or fourteen moonshines   5
> Lag of a brother? Why bastard? wherefore base?
> When my dimensions are as well compact,
> My mind as generous and my shape as true,
> As honest madam's issue? Why brand they us
> With base? with baseness? bastardy? base, base?   10
> Who in the lusty stealth of nature take
> More composition and fierce quality
> Than doth, within a dull, stale, tired bed,
> Go to th' creating a whole tribe of fops,
> Got 'tween asleep and wake? Well then,   15
> Legitimate Edgar, I must have your land:
> Our father's love is to the bastard Edmund
> As to the legitimate: fine word 'legitimate'!
> Well, my legitimate, if this letter speed,
> And my invention thrive, Edmund the base   20
> Shall top the legitimate. I grow; I prosper:
> Now, gods, stand up for bastards!

2-3   **Wherefore should I/Stand in the plague of custom:**
       why should I have to submit to the unjust laws of
       convention

3-4   **permit/The curiosity of nations to deprive me:**
       (why should I) allow the over-meticulous conventions
       of society to deprive me of my inheritance

5-6   For that I am some twelve ... a brother?:
simply because I was born twelve or fourteen months after my brother

6   bastard ... base:
both words mean an illegitimate, a bastard, born outside marriage

7   my dimensions are as well compact:
my body is as well formed

9   As honest madam's issue: as the child of a married woman

20-21   [if] my invention thrive, ... the legitimate:
if my plan works, Edmund the bastard shall take the place of the legitimate Edgar

22   stand up for bastards:
rise (everybody) for the cause of all bastards

Speech 2

"Hear, nature, hear; dear goddess, hear"

Background to the Story

King Lear has been king for many years and in order "to shake all cares and business from our age" he wishes to retire and hand over the control of the kingdom to his three daughters, Goneril, Regan and Cordelia. He proposes to make the division of his kingdom dependent upon the public declaration of each daughter's love for him.

Goneril, the wife of the Duke of Albany, declares before the assembled courtiers, earls and dukes, that she loves him "more than words can wield the matter". Regan, the wife of the Duke of Cornwall, professes that her love for him is such that she is only happy when she is in his "dear highness' love". These exaggerated protestations of love please the old king.

Cordelia who loves him sincerely is averse to making a public declaration of her love and incurs the anger of her father. He cuts her off from her share of the kingdom and divides it now between Goneril and Regan.

Once Goneril and Regan have inherited the kingdom they plan to stand firmly against their father and to rid him of all authority. Goneril begins by advising her servants to treat Lear with disrespect. She criticises the behaviour of the hundred knights, whom Lear has retained as his retinue, and reduces the number to fifty. This monstrous ingratitude of Goneril throws Lear into a passion of anger and he calls upon his goddess nature to make Goneril sterile and "dry up in her the organs of increase". If she does have a child, he prays that it will be "a thwart disnatured torment to her" and that it will "stamp wrinkles in her brow of youth". He wants his daughter Goneril to feel how sharp "a serpent's tooth it is to have a thankless child".

Character of the Speaker

Lear is the central figure around whom the whole play revolves. At the beginning of the play he is the embodiment of all that man looks for in life:

— he has wealth, family, many personal followers

— his reign has been successful

— he has been a good king, powerful, great and successful

— he has never known misfortune or misery.

But his very success as king brings about his downfall:

(a) He has become autocratic and choleric with an overbearing, domineering nature.

(b) He is now fiery and fierce in his attitude to life and in his actions.

(c) He is a dictator with a streak of arrogance in his disposition.

(d) He can tolerate no opposition to his decisions; he must have his way and expects everybody to quake at his words.

(e) He has been so used to command, so accustomed to bending others to his rule that he has now become self-centred, arrogant and haughty.

(f) His haughtiness has developed in him an ungovernable temper and rage which bursts forth, as it does in this speech, with disastrous consequences to others and particularly to himself.

Lear's Abdication

It was commonly thought in Shakespeare's day that all power and authority comes from God and that it is a sin to upset the established order. When man misuses the delegated authority of God, he brings disasters upon himself and the world around him. Viewed in this way, Lear has sinned doubly:

(a) He has resigned the responsibility of kingship.

(b) He has relinquished the natural authority of a father over his children.

Consequences of Lear's Sins:

— all the domestic problems of the play.

— Lear's own misery and unhappiness.

— the unfilial conduct of his daughters, Goneril and Regan.

— the banishment of his youngest daughter, Cordelia.

Important Points to Remember

It would be so easy to condemn Lear for his foolishness in abdicating and for his selfishness in demanding a public profession of love from his daughters, but we must remember:

— he was once a grand, noble and heroic king.

— he was a symbol of dignity.

— the outburst of his petulance against Cordelia and her banishment may have been the result of his great love for her; after all, she was his youngest daughter and unmarried.

    his own wife was dead and he has an intense desire to be loved, more particularly by his youngest daughter.

— he is old and his action is the action of a wayward old man and is most human.

Against Whom is the Speech Directed

Goneril, the eldest of Lear's daughters, has used her cunning and her flattery, to obtain power over her father. Once she has obtained it, she disparages her benefactor and calls attention to his lack of judgement in casting off Cordelia. In her eyes he is rash, wayward and infirm and her immediate plan is to take all power from him. She is not an ordinary wicked woman, who is bad on the spur of the moment and sorry afterwards: wickedness and disloyalty are part and parcel of her very nature. She is a detestable woman - hard, black in thought and in deed, with none of the female virtues. It is only now that Lear begins to realise this and this gives poignancy to the whole speech.

Speaking the Speech

The speaker therefore requires to be fiery and fierce, self-centred and arrogant, with an ungovernable temper. Yet the speech must be spoken with a slow, dreadful calm strength as Lear calls down upon Goneril the worst curse of the gods on any woman, sterility or a child of spleen. The speaker who rails and rants this passage is not interpreting Shakespeare properly.

Speech 2: "Hear, nature, hear; dear goddess, hear!"

LEAR

            Hear, nature, hear; dear goddess, hear!
Suspend thy purpose if thou didst intend
To make this creature fruitful;
Into her womb convey sterility;
Dry up in her the organs of increase,   5
And from her derogate body never spring
A babe to honour her! If she must teem,
Create her child of spleen, that it may live
And be a thwart disnatured torment to her!
Let it stamp wrinkles in her brow of youth;   10
With cadent tears fret channels in her cheeks;
Turn all her mother's pains and benefits
To laughter and contempt; that she may feel
How sharper than a serpent's tooth it is
To have a thankless child!   15

6   **her derogate body:** her degraded body

7   **If she must teem:** if she has children

9   **a thwart disnatured torment to her:**
     a perverse unnatural torture to her

11 **With cadent tears fret channels:**
     with tears falling continually, make channels (in her
     cheeks)

14 **serpent:** viper, symbol of ingratitude

Speech 3

"I am ashamed that thou hast power to shake my manhood thus"

Lear's Hopes to be Dashed

In speech 2 we heard Lear's invective against Goneril. He is seen suffering at the hands of a daughter whom he has not wronged: in return for his generosity he receives nothing but the grossest ingratitude. His whole manly frame shakes as he curses her whom he dearly loved and hot tears run down the cheeks of this once dignified king and father. It is a pathetic sight, and he himself is astonished at his own loss of dignity. He begins to feel pangs of remorse for what he has done to Cordelia and is aware that he is allowing passion to get the better of him. He tries to control himself and looks forward to support from his other daughter, Regan.

His Hopes

Lear hopes to receive kindness and comfort from Regan. He hopes that she will flay with her nails the wolfish face of Goneril and the thought gives him the strength of feeling that he will not lose control of himself - that he "will resume the shape" of authority as a king. But all his hopes are to be dashed: he is unaware that Regan is in league with Goneril in her opposition to him. She is just as blood-thirsty, evil-minded and suspicious as her sister, not as great a monster as Goneril, but with the power of casting more venom into her speech and actions.

Speaking the Speech

The speaker must feel like Lear. He must feel the emotion of his shaken manhood, his curses and his tears and his hopes for recovery.

Speech 3: "I am ashamed that thou has power"

LEAR

I am ashamed
That thou hast power to shake my manhood thus:
That these hot tears, which break from me perforce,
Should make thee worth them. Blasts and fogs upon thee!
Th' untented woundings of a father's curse   5
Pierce every sense about thee! Old fond eyes,
Beweep this cause again, I'll pluck ye out,
And cast you, with the waters that you loose,
To temper clay. Yea, is it come to this?
Ha! Let it be so; yet have I left a daughter,   10
Who, I am sure, is kind and comfortable.
When she shall hear this of thee, with her nails
She'll flay thy wolvish visage. Thou shalt find
That I'll resume the shape which thou dost think
I have cast off for ever.   15

4   **tears, which break from me perforce:**
     tears which are uncontrollable, forced out of me

5   **Th' untented woundings of a father's curse:**
     the deep (untreated) wounds you have caused your father
     make him curse you

8-9 **the waters that you loose,/To temper clay:**
     the tears that fall will moisten clay

13   **She'll flay thy wolvish visage:**
     she will scratch your face which is like a wolf's

14   **I'll resume the shape:**
     I will take upon myself the authority I had as a king

Speeches 4 and 5

"Blow, winds, and crack your cheeks!"
"Rumble thy bellyful! Spit, fire! spout, rain!"

Background to the Speeches

Act II ended with all the forces of darkness ranged against a poor, defenceless Lear. He is driven to the verge of insanity by the ingratitude of two daughters and gives vent to his feelings in violent curses, calling down "all the stored vengeances of heaven" upon his own flesh and blood. Act III scene ii, with a raging storm, adds its weight to the pathos of Lear's position:

(a) He is alone, deserted by all, except the Fool.

(b) He wanders across a treeless heath, bareheaded and drenched to the skin, on a stormy night of desolation.

(c) A pitiful, shivering Fool is at his side.

(d) The storm is at its height with its deluging streams, its fierce thrusts of lightning and the reverberating rumble of thunder.

The Storm in Nature

The poetry helps us to visualise the scene of a king flung from the highest elevation into the deepest abyss of misery - a king exposed to the fury of the wind and rain on a stormy lonely heath:

(a) the skies are wrathful.

(b) there are "sheets of fire", bursts of horrid thunder.

(c) we hear the groans of roaring winds and rain.

(d) the images pile up, painting the scene for us:

  — drenched steeples;

  — sulphurous fires;

  — oak-cleaving thunderbolts;

  — thunder-cracking nature's moulds;

  — spouting cataracts and hurricanoes.

Listen to the Poetry

It is not simply a description of a storm; it is the creation of a storm - creation by the power of its music, and the power of its imaginative suggestion.

Lear in the Storm

He is on the verge of insanity. He has suffered horribly at the hands of those he loved. But the agony of his spiritual torment is not powerful enough to make him absolutely insane. An external shock is needed to complete the shattering of the aged king's mind. The storm is the shock:

(a) The storm in nature is in sympathy with the storm in Lear's mind.

(b) The violence of the storm is a reflection of Lear's emotions and it helps us to understand his madness.

(c) The force of the storm's strength in nature reflects the chaos of a fallen king.

Lear has suffered so much agony within his own mind as a result of the ingratitude of his two daughters that he cannot feel the fury of the storm and he does not see anything wrong in nature behaving thus: "I tax not you, you elements, with unkindness". He is deeply moved by the storm, but it is the shock of ingratitude that brings him to the edge of madness.

He is not mad yet. His words still have sense and he is making great efforts to retain his sanity. He is trying so hard to be patient - patient with his daughters, patient with the storm: "I will be," he says, "the pattern of all patience". Perhaps he is trying too hard: the enormous effort is bound to take its toll and his mind will crack eventually.

We soon see the first symptoms of the altered attitude of Lear's mind:

(a)   He is intent on his mental agony.

(b)   He considers himself "a man more sinn'd against than sinning.

(c)   The autocratic, selfish father, now in his own mind, has become "a poor, infirm, weak and despised old man".

Speaking the Speeches

The speaker must:

(a)   endeavour to convey the tension and the torment in the mind of Lear.

(b)   study the vocabulary, the imagery, the rhythm of the verse and make himself one with the raging storm.

(c)   surrender as much of himself as he can in order to comprehend the character of Lear, and identify himself with him, and then allow the words and the poetry and the magic of the verse take over.

(d)   paint a picture of a defiant Lear, a Lear terribly great but at the same time pathetic and old by contrast with the elements.

Speech 4: "Blow, winds, and crack your cheeks! rage! blow!"

Speech 5: "Rumble thy bellyful! Spit, fire! Spout, rain!"

LEAR

                    Blow, winds, and crack your cheeks! rage!
blow!
You cataracts and hurricanoes, spout
Till you have drench'd our steeples, drown'd the cocks!
You sulphurous and thought-executing fires,
Vaunt-couriers of oak-cleaving thunderbolts,   5
Singe my white head! And thou, all-shaking thunder,
Strike flat the thick rotundity o' the world,
Crack nature's moulds, all germains spill at once,
That makes ingrateful man!

FOOL

                    O nuncle, court holy-water in a dry house 10
is better than this rain-water out o' door. Good nuncle,
in; ask thy daughters blessing: here's a night
pities neither wise men nor fools.

LEAR

     Rumble thy bellyful! Spit, fire! Spout, rain!
Nor rain, wind, thunder, fire are my daughters:
I tax not you, you elements, with unkindness.   15
I never gave you kingdom, called you children;
You owe me no subscription: then, let fall
Your horrible pleasure. Here I stand your slave,
A poor, infirm, weak, and despised old man.
But yet I call you servile ministers,   20

That will with two pernicious daughters join
Your high-engendered battles 'gainst a head
So old and white as this. O, O! 'tis foul!

2   **hurricanoes:** storms with violent winds

3   **drown'd the cocks:** drowned the weathercocks on buildings

4   **thought-executing fires:** lightning that is as swift as thought

5   **Vaunt-couriers of oak-cleaving thunderbolts:**
      forewarnings of thunder which split oak trees in two

7   **Strike flat the thick rotundity o' the world:**
      make the round world flat

8   **all germains spill at once:**
      destroy all seeds of nature at one blow

10   **court holy-water in a dry house:**
      look for flattery in a house without humour

13   **Rumble thy bellyful:** growl to your heart's content

16   **I tax not you, you elements, with unkindness:**
      I am not accusing you of being unkind

17   **You owe me no subscription:**
      you owe me no loyalty, no allegiance

20   **I call you servile ministers:** I call you slaves

22   **Your high engendered battles:**
      your armies that have been formed in the heavens

Speech 6

"Hold your hands in benediction o'er me"

Choice of Scene

As we approach the final stages of the play which is so packed full of eventful incidents it is difficult to select a scene to bring this section to a close:

(a) We could have the scene of Edmund's triumph, with the British forces conquering the French and see Lear and Cordelia as his prisoners.

(b) We could have the scene of the blinding of Gloucester with its blood-curdling savagery.

(c) We could have Edmund's trial by combat and his death with his wheel of fortune come full circle.

(d) We could have the scene of the wrangling between Goneril and Regan as they fight for the love of Edmund.

(e) We could have the heart-rending scene of Lear carrying in his arms the dead body of Cordelia and hear his agonised cry and feel the piteous agony of his yearning for her as he dies of a broken heart.

Choice of Speech

A difficult decision but my choice is the scene of the reconciliation between Lear and Cordelia. It is one of the most tender scenes ever written, with father and daughter together again after such a long separation and both willing to forgive and forget. It is a scene of tenderness, genuine love and sympathy.

Reconciliation between Father and Daughter

The picture of King Lear, fantastically dressed with flowers, uttering now strange sentences, now sublime thoughts, is a side-piercing sight. He was once "every inch a king" and is now a "ruined piece of nature", but convinced that he has still the power to inspire his subjects with awe and still the authority over life and death. He has been brought to this state by his suffering at the hands of his two daughters, Goneril and Regan.

His unsuspecting nature was:

— not able to penetrate their true natures.

— not able to see through their hypocrisy and deceit.

— too generous to suspect them.

When he finally comes to the full realisation of their devilish natures and his own utter folly in abdicating and surrendering all power to them, and particularly the folly of not seeing true love in the heart of the daughter he abandoned, the shock was terrific. He experiences bitterness of soul, struggled within his own mind for sanity, slips into temporary madness and then into complete insanity. It is a tragic picture of a once great king and father.

But all is not lost for him. He has suffered the purgatory of the mind in his awareness and acknowledgement of his own mistakes. Through suffering he has learnt the true nature of friendship, loyalty and love and at last is saved from complete despair by the forgiving and redeeming love of Cordelia.

Beautiful Picture of Forgiveness

Cordelia stands at his bedside with daughterly devotion. She is full of compassion and tenderness for her father, recalls the violent harm her two sisters have done to him and gives him a loving kiss of peace. He wakens and there is no anger or reprimand in her first words to him. With beautiful simplicity she addresses him:

"How fares your majesty?". We see tears of sorrow on the face of Lear for the daughter he disowned, a face that "opposed against the warring winds" of the storm and stood "against the deep dread bolted thunder". She does not complain of what he has done to her but asks his blessings: "hold your hand in benediction o'er me".

The heart-broken king tries to rise and kneel before her, acknowledging his past sins. She begs him not to kneel or weep. He is ready to end his life and drink the poison he thinks she has for him. He acknowledges that she has the right to revenge on him for the wrongs he has done her. Her reply is full of tender feeling: "No cause, no cause". She raises him up from the bed, puts fresh garments on him and they both leave the scene arm in arm. Lear has regained his sanity in the love and forgiveness of his daughter and she has regained a father.

Speech 6: "Hold your hand in benediction o'er me"

CORDELIA

Sir, do you know me?

LEAR

You are a spirit, I know. Where did you die?

CORDELIA

Still, still, far wide!

DOCTOR

He's scarce awake. Let him alone awhile.

LEAR

Where have I been? Where am I? Fair daylight?   5
I am mightily abused. I should e'en die with pity,
To see another thus. I know not what to say.
I will not swear these are my hands. Let's see -
I feel this pin prick. Would I were assured
Of my condition!

CORDELIA

O look upon me, sir.   10
And hold your hand in benediction o'er me.
No, sir, you must not kneel.

LEAR

Pray, do not mock me.
I am a very foolish fond old man,
Fourscore and upward, not an hour more nor less;
And, to deal plainly,   15
I fear I am not in my perfect mind.
Methinks I should know you, and I know this man;

Yet I am doubtful, for I am mainly ignorant
What place this is; and all the skill I have
Remembers not these garments; nor I know not   20
Where I did lodge last night. Do not laugh at me;
For, as I am a man, I think this lady
To be my child Cordelia.

CORDELIA

        And so I am! I am!

LEAR

Be your tears wet? Yes, 'faith. I pray, weep not;
If you have poison for me, I will drink it,   25
I know you do not love me, for your sisters
Have, as I do remember, done me wrong:
You have some cause, they have not.

CORDELIA

No cause, no cause.

6   **I am mightily abused:**
     I am not thinking straight, I am greatly deluded

14 **I am a very foolish fond old man:**
     I am a very foolish and silly old man

22 **all the skill I have/Remembers not these garments:**
     All the wit I have do not let me know where I got these
     clothes I am wearing

Questions

1. Can you see any good points in the character of Edmund?
    What are they?

2.   Is Edmund justified in what he intends to do? Has he been a
     victim of society?

3.   To what extent do you agree that Lear was "a man more sinn'd
     against than sinning"?

Memorable Lines

I, i:
                    "'tis our fast intent
To shake all cares and business from our age."

"Come not between the dragon and his wrath."

"The bow is bent and drawn; make from the shaft."

"My life I never held but as a pawn
To wage against thine enemies; nor fear to lose it."

                    "that glib and oily art,
To speak and purpose not."

                    "Love's not love
When it is mingled with regards that stand
Aloof from the entire point."

I, ii: "This is the excellent foppery of the world, that, when we
are sick in fortune - often the surfeit of our own
behaviour - we make guilty of our disasters the sun, the
moon and the stars, as if we were villains on necessity,
fools by heavenly compulsion, knaves, thieves and
treachers by sperical predominance, drunkards, liars and
adulterers, by an enforced obedience of planetary influence."

                    "a brother noble,
Whose nature is so far from doing harms
That he suspects none."

I, iv: "Ingratitude, thou marble-hearted fiend,
More hideous when thou show'st thee in a child
Than the sea monster!"

II, iv: "I abjure all roofs, and choose
To wage against the enmity o' the air;
To be a comrade with the wolf and owl -
Necessity's sharp pinch!"

"thou art a boil,
A plague-sore, an embossed carbuncle,
In my corrupted blood."

"touch me with noble anger,
And let not women's weapons, water-drops,
Stain my man's cheeks!"

III, ii: "I will be the pattern of all patience."

"I am a man
More sinn'd against than sinning."

III, iv: "Poor naked wretches, wheresoe'er you are,
That bide the pelting of this pitiless storm,
How shall your houseless heads and unfed sides,
Your loop'd and window'd raggedness, defend you
From seasons such as these?"

III, vi: "When we our betters see bearing our woes,
We scarcely think our miseries our foes
Who alone suffers, suffers most i' th' mind.
....
The mind much sufferance doth o'erskip,
When grief hath mates."

IV, i: "As flies to wanton boys, are we to the gods;
They kill us for their sport."

IV, ii: "Wisdom and goodness to the vile seem vile."

"Proper deformity shows not in the fiend
So horrid as in woman."

IV, vi: "Every inch a king."

"When we are born, we cry that we are come
To this great stage of fools."

V, i: "he's full of alteration
And self-reproving."

V, iii: "The wheel is come full circle."

                    "All friends shall taste
The wages of their virtue, and all foes
The cup of their deservings."

**"Were you in my stead, would you have heard
A mother less? or granted less?"**

*photograph on page 111
shows Laurence Olivier
as Coriolanus*

A Glance at

CORIOLANUS

Date of the Play

Coriolanus was possibly written in 1608 and published in 1623. It certainly belongs to the group of plays written after *Hamlet* (1603).

Play in Outline

There is a famine in Rome and the citizens rebel against the Senate and particularly against Caius Marcius. He is a soldier who has deserved worthily of his country but he has nothing but contempt for ordinary people. He upbraids them for daring to ask for privileges.

The Volsces are great rivals of the Romans and they plan to invade Rome. Marcius is summoned to battle against the leader of the Volsces, Tullus Aufidius. The siege of Corioli takes place and at first the Romans are repulsed. Marcius pursues the fleeing Volsces through the city gates and the soldiers hail him by the title Coriolanus.

His mother Volumnia is proud of her son's victory but his gentle wife Virgilia is afraid for his safety.

In the meantime the citizens in Rome have been granted the privilege of having tribunes to look after their interests. Two of them, Sicinius and Brutus, hate Coriolanus. He has been nominated to the office of Consul by the Senate and the two tribunes convince the fickle citizens that as Consul, he could deprive them of their liberties.

It was the custom in Rome for a nominated Consul to stand in the

Forum before the people, display his wounds of war and beg the votes of the citizens. In spite of his contempt for such a humiliating act, Coriolanus swallows his pride but eventually loses his temper. He is banished. As he leaves he curses Rome and leaves it defenceless.

Disguised as a beggar, Coriolanus goes to Antium. His rival Aufidius has been raising a new army against Rome. Coriolanus joins him and is made an equal in command. Both advance on Rome. Coriolanus is very popular with the troops. This makes Aufidius envious but he bides his time for vengeance.

The army reaches the gates of Rome and the Romans beg for mercy. Coriolanus is deaf to all their entreaties. He relents when his mother, his wife and his young son kneel before him. He withdraws his troops and returns to Corioli.

Aufidius accuses him of denying the Volsces a victory over the Romans and calls him a traitor. Coriolanus is stabbed by a hired conspirator. Aufidius is struck with sorrow and resolves to do honour to the glory and greatness of the memory of Coriolanus.

Style of the Play

The intellectual strain predominates over the poetical, the drama over the music. According to Professor Bradley, the style is heightened, grander, wilder, more swelling and sometimes, involved and obscure. But do not let this put you off the play, for it is a play full of life and movement and in the great passages, there are sudden, strange, electrifying effects which are rarely found in Shakespeare's plays.

It is a play of vehement passion and while the passion is not as gripping as that which we find in *King Lear* or *Othello*, the play has other qualities that are well worth our study. It is perhaps Shakespeare's greatest triumph in organisation, technically and artistically perfect, supreme in its completeness and effectiveness.

The genius of the dramatist can be seen in his skill in condensing, hastening, unifying, intensifying and supplementing the vigorous dramatic life that permeates the play.

A Different Kind of Play

(a) Do not be put off by the bareness of its style.

(b) Do not look for the undulating, heaving swell of language that you find in the music of *Othello*.

(c) Do not expect the compelling power of fireworks of *Julius Caesar* or the fine frenzies of *King Lear* or *Macbeth*.

Coriolanus is a different kind of play. It is a play:

(a) about Rome with its conflicts of patriotism and pride.

(b) dealing with the struggles between family affection on the one hand and the interest of revenge and egotism on the other.

(c) set in the world of hard weapons, civic brawls and the crash of war.

(d) of arguments for and against aristocracy or democracy, on liberty and slavery, on power and the abuse of it, on peace and war.

Such a play requires a verse powerful, rounded and resonant, borne forward by a compelling rhythm and a hero whose character, deeds and fate absorb our interest from the selected speeches.

Selection of Memorable Speeches

(1) "All the contagion of the south light on you"
     Act I, Scene iv, lines 30-42   (Marcus)

(2) "Better it is to die, better to starve"
     Act II, Scene iii, lines 108-119   (Coriolanus)

(3)   "I prithee now, my son"
      Act III, Scene ii, lines 72-86   (Volumnia)

(4)   "You common cry of curs"
      Act III, Scene iii, lines 121-136   (Coriolanus)

(5)   "O mother, mother! what have you done?"
      Act V, Scene iii, lines 182-193   (Coriolanus)

Speech 1

"All the contagion of the south light on you!"

State of Affairs

As the play begins Rome is not a very pleasant Rome. It is a time of famine and yet the store-houses are crammed full with grain. It is a time of mutiny of the ordinary citizens who are resolved to die rather than famish, and who, in addition to their demands for corn, want a say in the running of affairs in Rome. The ruling classes, the patricians, proud of their power, treat the plebeians as underdogs and refuse all of their demands. Conflict is the result.

To add to the problem, there is the threat of war: Titus Aufidius, the leader of the Volscians, has planned to capture as many Roman towns as possible. The Romans under the command of Cominius, Lartius and Marcius besiege the town of Corioli and are at first repulsed, until the hero, Caius Marcius, cursing craven troops, alone pursues the fleeing Volscians through their gates, and although wounded, takes the city. For this great military exploit Cominius confers on him Rome's honour, the surname of Coriolanus.

Character of the Speaker

To understand the importance of this speech of Marcius' it is essential to spend time considering the character of the man and the situation in which he finds himself. Try to visualise the scene:

(a) It is a scene full of action of battle with drums and colours betokening an army on the march.

(b) We hear the sound of alarums and trumpets and the sounding of parleys and retreats.

(c) We witness the swaying confusion of battle.

(d) We see a triumphant Aufidius urging on the Volscians.

(e) In the background the senators of Corioli are upon the walls of their towns urging their men to defy the Romans, to anticipate each new assault by a sortie.

(f) We are certain that Marcius has been bearing the brunt of the battle himself and understand his despair at seeing his men beaten back.

(g) It is understandable then when we hear him giving vent to his feelings of anger at the cowardice of his men, and calling them "shames of Rome", "souls of geese".

But to understand his anger more fully we must understand the man:

(a) He is now the acknowledged leader, admirable for his own valour and personal prowess in war.

(b) He is the mainstay of the army, the hope of Rome, and the flower of warriors.

(c) He is an arrogant and haughty leader, a man of tremendous force and ungovernable pride who bullies and abuses his soldiers.

(d) He castigates and cows his men to silence, looks upon them as "dissentious rogues" and "curs", considering them as lacking all discretions and "passing cowardly".

(e) He is an aristocrat at heart, indifferent to the people's hardships and blind to the righteousness of their demands. Little wonder, in the eyes of the citizens, he is "the chief enemy to the people".

(f) He is a solitary figure, a man who has cut himself off from contact with friends, and too detached from the problems of his fellowmen.

(g) His patriotism and his bravery are beyond question but what remains in doubt is the reason for it:

— Is it the love of fame itself?

— Is it the desire to serve his country?

— Is it pride of family?

— Is it simply to please his mother?

(h) He is proud and insolent, despising his soldiers because they have not the same ardour for war as he and because they fall short of his standards of valour.

(i) He is intolerant and at times intolerable, a martyr to his own cause and perhaps the least sympathetic of all Shakespeare's heroes. But we must not be too ready to condemn him and must try to understand his point of view.

(j) The citizens of Rome are justified in their grievances: they are hungry and have no rights and many of the patricians would have compromised in these matters. But Marcius was not a man for compromise. He believed that for the Senate to show "cares" for the people could be construed as "fears" on their part and that all concessions weaken the state.

(k) Such an attitude of mind has made him into the man he is. He is an individual soul in the midst of a struggle for municipal powers between the nobles and people of Rome and at the same time confronted with an attack from his deadly enemy, Aufidius. Both the honour of Rome and his own honour is at stake; but honour for Marcius is the ladder of his own reputation. His craving for it leads to his eventual tragedy.

Speech 1: "All the contagion of the south light on you"

MARCIUS

All the contagion of the south light on you!
You shames of Rome! you herd of - Boils and plagues
Plaster you o'er, that you may be abhorred
Farther than seen, and one infect another
Against the wind a mile! You souls of geese,   5
That bear the shapes of men, how have you run
From slaves that apes would beat! Pluto and hell!
All hurt behind! backs red, and faces pale
With flight and agued fear! Mend and charge home,
Or, by the fires of heaven, I'll leave the foe   10
And make my wars on you! Look to 't. Come on!
If you'll stand fast, we'll beat them to their wives,
As they us to our trenches. Follow me!

1   **All the contagion of the south light on you:**
    may all the infectious diseases come upon you

7   **Pluto and hell:**
    Pluto was the Roman god of the underworld

8   **All hurt behind:**
    any injuries you have received you got when you were
    running away from the enemy

8-9   **faces pale/With flight and agued fear!:**
    your retreat and shivering fits of fear (of the enemy) have
    made you all look pale

9   **Mend and charge home:**
    mend your ways and fight to the utmost, to the last man

Speech 2

"Better it is to die, better to starve"

Background to the Speech

During the siege of Corioli, Marcius distinguishes himself in single-handed exploits. His valour is crowned with the title of Coriolanus. He returns to Rome in triumph, wearing the war's oaken garland and bearing the new name. The Senate, recognising the services he has rendered to Rome in defeating the Volscians, nominates him to the high honour of the office of Consul.

But there is a problem: according to custom the hero has still to seek favour with the ordinary people - custom demands that they have to give their consent to the nomination. Custom also demands that the nominee:

(a)   should stand in the Forum and publicly display his wounds of battle.

(b)   should don the gown of humility.

(c)   should humbly beg the votes of the citizens.

For Coriolanus this is a major problem:

(a)   He would be forced to strip himself of his material trappings, the oaken garland of war, and to wear a gown of humility.

(b)   He would have to compromise with the custom of the times.

(c)   He would have to bend the knee and flatter the very citizens who had fled from the enemy, by begging their votes.

The Problem for Coriolanus

(a)   He is an exceptional man, an aristocrat by birth, temperament and nature.

(b) He is proud, but his pride is for greatness, for honour, for Rome and for the aristocracy.

(c) His philosophy of life is that the patricians are the bulwarks of the social order.

(d) He proves himself to be a hero, a superhuman warrior on the battlefield, and alone and blood-stained and single-handed he enters the gates of Corioli and defeats the enemy.

(e) His boldness and strength makes the enemy shake with his "grim looks and the thunder-like percussion of sounds".

(f) He watches his own men flee from the fight and he loathes them for it and now he is expected to beg favours from them.

His soldier's pride disgusts him at the thought of the masquerade of pretended humility. He is more used to action in battle than reasoning coolly with himself or with others and feels that it is distasteful and against his convictions to have to bow to custom. He has contempt for the very people from whom he must now beg favours: better now to die and starve than submit to craving the hire which he rightly deserves.

The problem for Coriolanus is:

— is he to stand firm in his convictions?

— is he to humiliate himself?

— is he to let the high office and honour go, or, is he the noble, high-ranking commander ready to submit to the custom of simple folk who are only exercising their privileges?

Only he alone can decide and we realise how difficult the decision is for him. He is not used to indecisions or introspection and here we see him like an animal caught in a net, frantic, struggling. Whatever he decides to do is bound to release forces that will ultimately destroy him.

He has no political ambitions of his own but there is his mother to consider: she has high ideals for him. And there are the tribunes, no friends of his, who are politically shrewd and are bound to resort to all the tricks of their political trade and go to work on the ignorance (bordering on stupidity) of the people. For the moment Coriolanus feels powerless against such odds and this very fact fills us with pity and terror and overwhelms us with a sense of sadness at the waste of a good man and a good life. On the point of letting the high office and honour go, much against his will and conviction, he falls in with the advice of Menenius and goes through the ceremony of requesting the people's votes. But he does so with obvious ill-grave.

Speech 2: "Better it is to die, better to starve"

CORIOLANUS

Better it is to die, better to starve,
Than crave the hire which first we do deserve.
Why in this wolvish toge should I stand here,
To beg of Hob and Dick that does appear
Their needless vouches? Custom calls me to 't.   5
What custom wills, in all things should we do 't,
The dust on antique time would lie unswept
And mountainous error be too highly heaped
For truth t' o'erpeer. Rather than fool it so,
Let the high office and the honour go   10
To one that would do thus. I am half through;
The one part suffered, the other will I do.

2   **crave the hire which first we do deserve:**
        humiliate myself by begging for the consulship, which
        I deserve by my own military exploits

3   **Why in this wolvish toge should I stand here?:**
        why in this humiliating gown have I to stand here

4-5   **To beg of Hob and Dick ... vouches:**
        to beg useless votes from ordinary people like Tom,
        Dick or Harry, who have just turned up for the cere-
        mony

9   **Rather than fool it so:**
        rather than be a fool and agree to this

9-10   **Let the high office ... would do thus:**
        let the honour of consulship go to someone who would
        do this

11-12   **I am half through ... the other will I do:**
        I am half way through this ceremony and have had to
        put up with it; the other part, of humiliating myself, I will
        do

Speech 3

"I prithee now, my son"

A Crisis for the Hero

Coriolanus has been acclaimed by all the gentry of Rome as their Lord Consul but he is still faced with what for him is an insurmountable problem: to accept the bitter pill of the tribune's demand:

— to submit himself to the people's voices.

— to suffer the lawful censure for any of his human faults.

We can well imagine how the hero feels about this humiliation, a soldier of ungovernable pride and anger, who is aware of the tribune's plot to discredit him in the eyes of the people and who have called him "a foe to the public weal". They have accused him of robbing the citizens of their liberties and declared him worthy of death.

He has held firmly to an unpopular faith, the right of the patricians to govern, and the danger of giving privileges to the citizens. He has warned them that in soothing the plebeians, the patricians are nourishing the cockle of rebellion, insolence and sedition. But they refuse to listen to him or to protect him from the outrage of a public submission to people whom he has served so well on the battlefield and in return has to accept a public censure for human faults, which are as common to his accusers as they are to him.

It is a crisis for him. A little guile, a little deceit, would win him the favour of the people. He could so easily deceive them with false promises and dissemble his nature. But he hates his own people with such intensity that it verges on monomania. In his attitude to the crisis which is to make him or break him he shows class-pride and the lack of well-tempered virtue. As we watch him we may feel angry with him for his inability to cope with the final round of a political struggle and we wonder what will be the attitude of his mother.

The Hero's Mother

In the delineation of the character of Volumnia, Shakespeare has carved in deathless marble a figure of a typical Roman matron:

(a) She is majestic and imposing, full of the virtues and prejudices of her class.

(b) She is strong and dignified and her feeling of devotion to her country outweighs her maternal instincts.

(c) She has sent her son to cruel wars to find fame. She has rejoiced in his prowess and in his wounds.

(d) She has been all along the guiding influence for her son; from her he has inherited her pride, her scorn of the mass of the people, and her heroic grandeur of bearing.

(e) He has been an invincible soldier but is vulnerable before her powerful will and her strong influence on his life and powers of decisions have stultified his independent manhood.

(f) A crisis is the real test of character: it brings out the best or the worst in a man or a woman. In the crisis that faces Coriolanus we see how pride and passion have hardened the very nature of Volumnia.

Clash of Personalities

Act III scene ii and this speech of Volumnia's ("I prithee now, my son") give us a clear picture of the clash of personalities of mother and son. The whole force of the impression of the play at this part is not merely a debate between hero and the Roman mob, or a conflict between the patricians and the plebeians: it is a match of passion played out for life and death between a mother and her son. She:

— has been the driving force throughout his life.

— is the mother with political ambitions for her son.

— has flattered him and made a soldier of him.

— has been responsible for his pride and now, when the moment of honour comes his way and just requires a simple act of humility on his part, she cannot control his pride. (Coriolanus cannot understand his mother's present disapproval of his uncompromising attitude towards the citizens and the tribunes.)

— advises him to swallow his indignities and make a humble appearance before the people and listen to their censure of his faults. (He is greatly disturbed - he has to decide either to be true to himself or to run the risk of losing her love.)

It is a time of deep mental anguish for the hero of the play. She is counselling him to follow a course of action against his nature and he rebels. She piles on arguments, insisting that she would use dissimulation to achieve an end, reprimands him for his behaviour and hints at her own agony of soul. Finally, she imposes her will upon him.

In this speech Volumnia is coaxing Coriolanus to be false to his native integrity of soul and we see the struggle going on in his soul. It is a speech of a mother who knows every trick of the trade in her dealings with her son.

Speech 3: "I prithee now, my son"

VOLUMNIA

                    I prithee now, my son,
Go to them, with this bonnet in thy hand;
And thus far having stretched it - here be with them -
Thy knee bussing the stones - for in such business
Action is eloquence, and the eyes of th' ignorant   5
More learned than the ears - waving thy head,
Which, often thus correcting thy stout heart,
Now humble as the ripest mulberry
That will not hold the handling; or say to them
Thou art their soldier, and being bred in broils   10
Hast not the soft way which, thou dost confess,
Were fit for thee to use as they to claim,
In asking their good loves; but thou wilt frame
Thyself, forsooth, hereafter theirs, so far
As thou hast power and person.   15

2   **Go to them, with this bonnet in thy hand:**
         take off your hat before them as a sign of your humility

4   **Thy knees bussing the stones:**
         let your knees kiss the ground before them

5   **Action is eloquence:**
         actions speak louder than words - what they see is all
         important

5-6   **th' eyes of the ignorant ... more learned than the ears:**
         uneducated people think more of what they see than
         what they hear

6-7   **thy head,/Which, often thus correcting thy stout
         heart:**
         your intelligent mind does not give you the desire to do
         this

8   **Now humble as the ripest mulberry:**
> in front of the common people be as humble as the ordinary mulberry tree

10   **being bred in broils:**
> more used to struggles in battle than the use of words

11   **Hast not the soft way:**
> (tell them you) are not used to the soft words of pleading with people

13-14   **thou wilt frame/Thyself, forsooth, hereafter theirs:**
> promise them that in future you will be gracious to them

Speech 4

"You common cry of curs"

Aftermath of the Clash

In speech 3 we witness the clash between the two personalities of mother and son. She rouses his anger by questioning his affection for her, telling him that it causes her as much dishonour to beg from him as it does him now to have to beg the favour of the people. He has performed bloody, pitiless deeds of war in order to feel loved by her and now to retain her love she is asking him to flatter people whom he despises.

At first he refuses to follow her advice, then agrees, then questions the wisdom of it, but finally surrenders. But the end of the clash is not the end of his problems. The power of the tribunes is growing daily and they are plotting to discredit Coriolanus in the eyes of the people:

(a) They call him a traitorous innovator, a foe to the public weal.

(b) They accuse him of robbing the citizens of their liberties.

(c) They declare that he is worthy of death.

Reaction of the Hero

It is all too much for him to bear. He flouts at the tribunes who are the mouthpiece of the mob. He calls them time-pleasers, flatterers, foes to nobleness. He could so easily have won over the citizens by apologising to them and acknowledging their part in the running of state affairs: citizens are as much a part of the state as those who govern. But his pride takes possession of him and his anger explodes like a rocket. He forgets the promise he made to his mother. He insults the citizens in a speech unequalled in the energy of its hatred. He curses Rome and its citizens and banishes himself from it, leaving it defenceless before its threatening enemies.

Speech 4: "You common cry of curs"

CORIOLANUS

> You common cry of curs, whose breath I hate
> As reek o' th' rotten fens, whose loves I prize
> As the dead carcasses of unburied men
> That do corrupt my air, I banish you!
> And here remain with your uncertainty.   5
> Let every feeble rumour shake your hearts!
> Your enemies, with nodding of their plumes,
> Fan you into despair! Have the power still
> To banish your defenders, till at length
> Your ignorance - which finds not till it feels,   10
> Making but reservation of yourselves,
> Still your own foes - deliver you as most
> Abated captives to some nation
> That won you without blows! Despising,
> For you, the city, thus I turn my back.   15

1   **You common cry of curs:**
     you vulgar pack of worthless dogs

1-2   **whose breath I hate/As reek o' th' rotten fens:**
     he despises the smell of their breath which reminds him of the smell of rotten vapour from the fens

5   **here remain with your uncertainty:**
     (there are several uncertainties about these two lines) Coriolanus is uncertain about the wisdom of seeking the votes of common people; citizens are uncertain about accepting him as Consul; the future of the citizens is now uncertain as he is banished

8-9   **Have the power still/To banish your defenders:**
     (there is a tinge of sarcasm in this remark) Coriolanus knows that in banishing him the citizens of Rome will have no one to defend them

10-12   **Your ignorance ... your own foes:**
Coriolanus tells them they will only realise their mistakes when Rome is attacked; their actions are making them enemies to themselves

11   **Making but reservations of yourselves:**
in banishing him the Romans are not even sparing themselves

11-12   **deliver you as most/Abated captives:**
(your ignorance) will make you all humble prisoners

15   **thus I turn my back:**
Coriolanus is banishing himself, turning his back on his country

Speech 5

"O mother, mother! What have you done?"

It requires great effort on the part of Coriolanus to put aside for a moment his pride and endeavour to placate the citizens of Rome by abiding by their little customs and thus win their "voices". However, the tribunes have been plotting to entrap the guileless soldier and their charge that he is a potential tyrant provokes him to another outburst. He is banished and now becomes a man dedicated to implacable vengeance. He has been rejected by Rome and his pride swells to a mountainous bulk full of resentment with a determination to "see Rome embraced with fire".

His decision to turn traitor to the Rome that has nourished his greatness may not win our sympathy but we must remember that he has fought and won great battles on behalf of Rome and now he is plotting against and betrayed by his fellow citizens, dis-crowned and stripped of his heroism. He has been an outstanding soldier, with devotion to ideals, indifferent to the consequences of his devotion, and with absolute personal disinterestedness, and for all this he is now banished.

We can understand how all the pent-up wrath within him produces a blind resolve to be revenged on those who have made him now a spectacle of fallen greatness. Banishment for him means separation from his mother, his wife and child and we can understand the agony that produces "my birthplace hate I, my love's upon this enemy town".

The Returned Warrior

The attack on Rome has begun. The Volscian army now under the leadership of Coriolanus and Aufidius has reached the gates of Rome. Comenius and Menenius plead for mercy but Coriolanus is deaf to all their entreaties. He yields a little by offering them their lives for the surrender of Rome but vows that he will not lend an ear to any further embassies.

However, the sight of his wife, mother and child paralyses him, and he experiences a new conflict in his soul as his pride and prejudice struggle with his sense of love and friendship.

Once again we have the clash between the determined man and the strong-willed mother:

— He is the rock, the oak not to be wind-shaken.

— She is the saviour of Rome, which will be lost unless she can force her will upon her son.

Coriolanus Faced with Mother, Wife and Child

(a) They look at him with "dove's eyes".

(b) He struggles to repress the upsurge of feelings of tenderness at the sight of his mother bowing to him and his young son with an "aspect of tenderness".

(c) He masters his feelings of tenderness and swears he will never "be such a gosling to obey instinct".

(d) His wife speaks to him and his resolution fails. He begs her to forgive his "tyranny".

(e) He calls his mother "the most noble mother of the world" but struggles not to listen to her presence.

(f) His mother gives him two alternatives:

— to destroy Rome.

— be led, as a foreign miscreant, with manacles through our streets.

(g) She plays on his affections: "show a noble grace" or tread "on thy mother's womb".

(h)   She kneels before him and he cannot stand the mental conflict against the sacred laws of nature.

(i)   She taunts him with being a traitor and a Volscian. The attack on his loyalty breaks him and he agrees to withdraw his armies from Rome.

(j)   In yielding to his mother, he is playing into the hands of his enemy Aufidius and is sealing his own doom. But once the decision has been taken, Coriolanus has no misgivings about broken pledges to allies. His death is almost instantaneous; it is needless but heroic. He dies not as a martyr to retrieved patriotism but as a victim to his own passion, pride and fiery temper. His death is poignant and pitiful: he is a traitor once again, not this time to Rome but to the Volscian cause.

Mood for the Speech

As the play comes to a fitting close, and this speech, in a way, prepares us for this, you must:

— place yourself in the mood of the speech.

— endeavour to experience some of the hero's struggle between family affection on the one hand and the interest of revenge and egotism on the other.

— feel the hero's agony of soul as he listens to his mother's appeal, her taunts and attacks on his personal loyalty.

— see the tears of a loved wife and the high spirits of a son.

— be lost for words and then driven forward to shatter the silence by one of the most powerful utterances in all drama: "O mother, mother! what have you done?".

Speech 5: "O mother, mother! What have you done?"

CORIOLANUS

[Coriolanus] holds her by the hand, silent.

O mother, mother!

What have you done? Behold, the heavens do ope,
The gods look down, and this unnatural scene
They laugh at. O my mother, mother! O!
You have won a happy victory to Rome;   5
But for your son - believe it, O believe it! -
Most dangerously you have with him prevailed,
If not most mortal to him. But let it come.
Aufidius, though I cannot make true wars,
I'll frame convenient peace. Now, good Aufidius,   10
Were you in my stead, would you have heard
A mother less? or granted less, Aufidius?

2   **the heavens do ope:**
> the heavens open (and look down on the scene of a mother, wife and child begging Coriolanus not to attack Rome)

7   **Most dangerously you have with him prevailed:**
> (he tells them) they have been successful in making him change his mind about attacking Rome and that he knows the folly of such a move

8   **If not most mortal to him:**
> the danger could result in his death

But let it come: let happen what is to happen

10   **I'll frame convenient peace:**
> I will make arrangements for suitable peace-terms

11   **Were you in my stead:**
> if you had been in my place (he tells Aufidius)

Questions

1. Is Coriolanus justified in his contempt for the people?

2. "Instead of enlisting our sympathy for the hero, Shakespeare deliberately alienates it." Consider this statement and refer to particular lines in the selected speeches in which the dramatist weighs the scales against the hero.

3. Comment on the statement that Volumnia virtually destroys her son.

4. What is the flaw in the hero's character that makes him fail as a tragic hero?

Memorable Lines

I, iv: "Put your shields before your hearts, and fight
With hearts more proof than shields."

II, i: "Nature teaches beasts to know their friends."

" ... one that converses more with the buttock of the night than with the forehead of the morning."

II, ii: " ... he hath so planted his honours in their eyes and their actions in their hearts that for their tongues to be silent and not confess so much were a kind of ingrateful injury."

II, iii: " ... for the multitude to be ingrateful, were to make a monster of the multitude."

III, i: "Put not your worthy rage into your tongue."

" ... manhood is called foolery when it stands
Against a falling fabric."

"His nature is too noble for the world."

"His heart's his mouth.
What his breast forges, that his tongue must vent."

III, ii: "I have a heart as little apt as yours,
But yet a brain that leads my use of anger
To better vantage."

" ... when extremities speak, I have heard you say,
Honour and policy, like unsevered friends,
I' th' war do grow together."

"I would dissemble with my nature where
My fortunes and my friends at stake required
I should do so in honour."

"I know thou hadst rather
Follow thine enemy in a fiery gulf
Than flatter him in a bower."

IV, i: " ... extremities was the trier of spirits."

IV, iii: " ... the fittest time to corrupt a man's wife is when she's
fall'n out with her husband."

IV, v: "thy face
Bears a command in 't."

IV, vi: "He leads them like a thing
Made by some other deity than nature."

IV, vii: "He'll be to Rome
As is the osprey to the fish, who takes it
By sovereignty of nature."

V, iv: "There is more mercy in him than there is milk in a male
tiger."

"The tartness of his face sours ripe grapes. When he
walks, he moves like an engine and the ground shrinks
before his treading."

"The potent poison quite o'er-crows my spirit.
... the rest is silence."

*photograph on page 141
shows Michael Pennington
as Hamlet*

A Glance at

HAMLET

Date of the Play

Some of Shakespeare's greatest tragedies were written in the period 1600-1608:

Hamlet	: 1600-1604
Othello	: 1604
King Lear	: 1605
Macbeth	: 1606
Coriolanus	: 1608

Outline of the Play

Hamlet is summoned back to court on the death of his royal father. Claudius, his uncle, seizes the throne, and marries Hamlet's mother, Gertrude. The hasty marriage adds to Hamlet's sorrow.

In an encounter with the Ghost of his father that stalks the battlements of the Castle, Hamlet learns the dreadful truth that Claudius has murdered his father. There is the duty of avenging the murder.

Hamlet was in love with Ophelia, the daughter of Polonius. On the advice of her father she repulses his advances and Hamlet feigns insanity. Claudius sets Rosencrantz and Guildenstern to spy upon Hamlet.

Hamlet invites strolling Players to present a murder play containing episodes resembling those of the actual killing of his father.

Rosencrantz and Guildenstern fail to discover the true cause of Hamlet's distraction, his pretended madness. Claudius decides to send Hamlet to England to have him killed there. He also sends two spies to keep an eye on him.

During the presentation of the murder play, Claudius is greatly disturbed but still Hamlet cannot make up his mind to kill him when he finds him at prayer.

Queen Gertrude upbraids Hamlet for his conduct. He turns upon her and she cries for help. There is a movement behind a curtain and Hamlet thinks it is Claudius spying there. He kills the object behind the curtain: it turns out to be Polonius. The Ghost appears again.

Hamlet escapes on his journey to England and lands in Denmark. The death of Polonius drives Ophelia insane. Laertes, Ophelia's brother, returns from Paris, to avenge his father's death. Claudius plots along with Laertes to kill Hamlet with a   poisoned rapier in a fencing match. Ophelia is drowned.

At the burial of Ophelia, Hamlet and Laertes fight. A duel is arranged between them. During the fight they accidently exchange rapiers. Laertes wounds Hamlet and   Hamlet wounds Laertes. Queen Gertrude drinks the poisoned wine which Claudius has prepared for Hamlet. With their dying lips, Gertrude and Laertes reveal the villainy of the King. Hamlet kills him. Hamlet dies from the wound he receives from Laertes' poisoned rapier.

Meaning of the Play

Shakespearean scholars throughout the ages have given serious thought to the meaning of the play: scholars such as Goethe, Coleridge and Bradley, and it is helpful to read what they say and feel about it. But to make our study worthwhile it is important for us to arrive at our own meaning. What makes the study so fascinating is that the play is modern in its problems and outlook and has a meaning for each and everyone of us, provided we face up to the problems. For we are all Hamlets and in him we can see a picture of ourselves.

Hamlet is a young man, lonely in spite of being a Prince of Denmark, a sensitive young man who is determined to take a stand in life against the corruption that surrounds him. He sees:

— his royal father meet an untimely death.

— himself denied the inheritance of the throne.

— his uncle achieve the glamour of his father's kingdom by suspect methods.

— himself standing by, concerned enough to question everything, and refusing to accept any enticing half-truths, but unable to become totally involved because of his own inner problems and nature.

Hamlet's tragedy is the tragedy of modern times and in it we can see a meaning for ourselves. It can be the tragedy of our:

— own spiritual powerlessness.

— own deadened energies.

— desire to do good in life and yet see ourselves with paralysed wills and aware of our own ineffectiveness.

The Significance of the Play

The play does not deal with an accurate historical record of a past event but it gives us the opportunity of living through a profound experience of a young man who is called upon to avenge a father's death and who in the process has to cut himself off from those who love him or those whom he loves. It is a serious problem for any young man and as we watch and suffer with him, as he faces up to this problem, perhaps his procrastination strikes a familiar chord in our own deepest nature. He looks for excuses, for ways out of facing up to his problems and in doing so creates so many other greater problems. He comes face to face with an evil force in life as symbolised by his uncle Claudius and revenge seems to be a way out for him and, what is more, a duty. But his noble mind will not allow him to take action, and his delay brings suffering and tragedy to himself and all those closely associated with him.

The Influence of Fate

The Greeks portrayed man bewildered, powerless in coping with life, pitted against some unknown power. But Hamlet is not a mere pawn, moved here, there and everywhere by some supreme power: he has free will, the freedom to act or not to act - the decision is his entirely. He is an agent in the hands of the gods but he can also be a victim when he opposes that power. He is not a mere puppet controlled by some whim of fate, but a living person, a rational being at the centre of the conflict between predestination and free will. That is what makes his contest and his tragedy so interesting.

We, like Hamlet, all have problems in our daily lives and fate, time, accident, has each its part to play - and this can be most frustrating. We have the day-to-day chores, the surrounding violence, the drugs, the examinations, the mortgages, the problems of our own natures and so we can sympathise with him and learn from him.

But Hamlet, unlike us, has to cope with another problem, the ghost of his dead father. Even in death this royal father wishes to be involved in structuring his son's future life and Hamlet finds himself driven by impulses emanating from his father's ghost, without the power to question the rationality of these impulses. His father in life and in death has an enormous influence on him for good or for evil. Perhaps here again we can see some relevance to our lives.

Selection of Memorable Speeches

(1) "O, that this too too sullied flesh would melt"
    Act I, Scene ii, lines 129-159.   (Hamlet)

(2) "Give thy thoughts no tongue"
Act I, Scene iii, lines 59-80.   (Polonius)

(3) "To be, or not to be"
Act III, Scene i, lines 56-90.   (Hamlet)

(4) "Now might I do it par"
Act III, Scene iii, lines 73-96.   (Hamlet)

"How all occasions do inform against me.
(5) Act IV, Scene iv, lines 32-66.   (Hamlet)

Speech 1

"O, that this too too sullied flesh would melt"

Facets of Hamlet's Character

The whole story of the play revolves around Hamlet and it is important therefore for us to get a glimpse into the heart of Hamlet, hear something of his secret thoughts, and even as early as Act I scene ii, experience a close emotional touch with them:

(a)   He is a very emotional young man. It is natural for any loving son to be sad at the death of a father, but here we see Hamlet overwhelmed with grief at the death of his father.

(b)   He is reflective by habit and intellectual by nature, more suited to the life of cultured ease as a student at the University of Wittenberg, the home of philosophical studies, than to the life of a man of action needed at the Court of Denmark. In his grief for his father he seems to revel in the thought of death and longs for death himself: "that this too too sullied flesh would melt".

(c)   He has even considered suicide as a way out of his grief but the only thing that stands between him and suicide is his deep sense of religious awe; he almost regrets that the "Everlasting" has "fixed his canon 'gainst self-slaughter".

(d)   He is by nature given to periods of melancholy. His present sadness is not simply for the particular reason of weariness of life in which he sees all life as "weary, stale, flat and unprofitable" and the entire world as "an unweeded garden that grows a seed".

(e)   He is a young man of excessive sensibility. Many a young man's mother has re-married but Hamlet is pierced to the soul by his mother's re-marriage. He explodes with a mixture of anger and disgust at the very thought of the speed with which his mother posted "with such dexterity to incestuous sheets". Her re-marriage is for him an enormous moral shock.

(f)   This shock prods him on to condemning the sensuality of all women in general: "Frailty, thy name is woman".

(g)   He is not a man given to action. We get the feeling that even now he has misgivings about the methods by which his uncle Claudius obtained the throne, but we know that he is not going to do anything about it: at least for the moment, or for many moments. For him there is a way out, a refuge in silence: "I must hold my tongue". Even though the whole thing has made him distraught, he is convinced that no action on his part will have any influence on future events. We know how wrong he is in this: thought, not action becomes the most important element in his life, and too much thought results in procrastination. When the moment for action is needed, in the very energy of his resolve there is a loss of power, or it is the wrong kind of action.

Speaking the Speech

—   Get yourself into the mood of the speech by thinking over the many facets of the character of Hamlet.

—   Be aware that you stand out in great contrast to the rest of the Court who are suitably dressed for the occasion of a marriage feast.

—   Unlike them, you are dressed in a suit of "solemn black" and you are "dejected".

—   You come on the stage, slowly, reluctantly.

Speech 1: "O, that this too too sullied flesh would melt"

HAMLET

<blockquote>
O, that this too too sullied flesh would melt,
Thaw, and resolve itself into a dew,
Or that the Everlasting had not fixed
His canon 'gainst self-slaughter. O God, God,
How weary, stale, flat, and unprofitable   5
Seem to me all the uses of this world!
Fie on 't, ah, fie, 'tis an unweeded garden
That grows to seed. Things rank and gross in nature
Possess it merely. That it should come to this,
But two months dead, nay, no so much, not two,   10
So excellent a king, that was to this
Hyperion to a satyr, so loving to my mother
That he might not beteem the winds of heaven
Visit her face too roughly. Heaven and earth,
Must I remember? Why, she would hang on him   15
As if increase of appetite had grown
By what it fed on, and yet within a month -
Let me not think on 't; frailty, thy name is woman -
A little month, or ere those shoes were old
With which she followed my poor father's body   20
Like Niobe, all tears, why she, even she -
O God, a beast that wants discourse of reason
Would have mourned longer - married with my uncle,
My father's brother, but no more like my father
Than I to Hercules. Within a month,   25
Ere yet the salt of most unrighteous tears
Had left the flushing in her galled eyes,
She married. O, most wicked speed, to post
With such dexterity to incestuous sheets!
It is not nor it cannot come to good.   30
But break my heart, for I must hold my tongue.
</blockquote>

3-4   **Or that the Everlasting ... 'gainst self-slaughter:**
        it is a pity that suicide is against the law of God

6   **all the uses of this world:**
        all the customs of this world

7   **Fie on 't:** an expression of disgust

11-12   **So excellent a king ... Hyperion to a satyr:**
        Hamlet's father was so "excellent" he was like the sun,
        and his uncle is like a "satyr", a Roman god in human
        form, with the ears and tail of a horse

12-14   **so loving to my mother ... her face too roughly:**
        Hamlet's father so loved his wife he would not allow her
        to go out in the rough weather

20-21   **she followed my poor father's body,/Like Niobe, all
        tears:**
        Niobe had six sons, six daughters. Leto, the mother of
        Apollo, slew all twelve of them. Niobe begged Jupiter
        to turn her into stone, which continued to shed tears of
        sorrow

25   **no more like my father/Than I to Hercules:**
        Hercules was the son of Jupiter and Alcemene. He was
        famous for his strength and exploits

26   **most unrighteous tears:**
        insincere tears

28-29   **to post/With such dexterity to incestuous sheets:**
        to hurry with such speed into an illegal marriage

31   **I must hold my tongue:** I must remain silent

Speech 2

"Give thy thoughts no tongue"

Background to the Speech

On the surface we are presented with a picture of an ordinary cheerful little family of three who enjoys the festivities of a marriage feast of a King and his Queen. There is the father, Polonius; a son, Laertes; and a daughter, Ophelia.

The marriage feast is over and Laertes is keen to return to his life in France. He is a pleasure-loving, wild and demoralised young man but his own way of life does not prevent him from moralising to his younger sister and pontificating about his knowledge of the ways of the world. He is a full-blooded, confident young man, vigorous in his attitude to life but very shallow in his thoughts.

His father has occupied a high place in the Government of his country, and has been zealous in the discharge of his duties. But he is obsequious and loquacious and certainly over-confident about his own ability. He is aware of his son's excesses in drinking, swearing, fencing and quarrelling and has accepted all this provided no scandals comes to the family - so unlike many other fathers in today's world.

It is an ordinary family scene of a brother taking leave of a sister before his departure and of a father giving his son some words of wisdom and advice before he leaves. But beneath the outside aspect of the scene we catch a glimpse of the ordinary courtiers who are now surrounding the throne of Denmark. They have accepted without question the explanation of Claudius for his hasty marriage and for the death of their former king. Surely there should have been some questions asked, some doubts and suspicions. Without these we can have a very corrupt society.

But for the moment this ordinary little family seems so secure in their good fortunes. Very soon they will all three of them be caught and broken in the drama of life. But for the moment too all we can do is listen to Polonius and his injunctions to his son.

A Quick Look at Polonius

(a) He has a considerable share of worldly wisdom about the rules of conduct in life.

(b) He can discuss how to behave with friends, how to behave in a quarrel, how to dress, how to deal with pecuniary loans.

(c) He is a man of maxims, so admirable in giving the general rules of life but such a dotard in advising his son and daughter on how to apply these to particular situations.

(d) He is consumed with conceit about his own intelligence and experience. But the advice he gives so easily, he is not able to follow himself. He advises Laertes "give thy thoughts no tongue". His own life at Court gives "tongue" to all his thoughts.

(e) He is a martinet. He rules the family with a rod of iron and demands ready obedience from them.

(f) His concern for his children is from a selfish point of view. It is not concern for their welfare but rather a selfish desire to prevent the scandal of a bad name on the family; that would make him look foolish in the eyes of the other courtiers.

(g) In spite of the weak points in his character his advice is clear, terse, sound and full of worldly wisdom.

Speech 2: "Give thy thoughts no tongue"

POLONIUS

> Give thy thoughts no tongue,
> Nor any unproportioned thought his act.
> Be thou familiar, but by no means vulgar.
> Those friends thou hast, and their adoption tried,
> Grapple them unto thy soul with hoops of steel,   5
> But do not dull thy palm with entertainment
> Of each new-hatched, unfledged courage. Beware
> Of entrance to a quarrel; but being in,
> Bear 't that th' opposed may beware of thee.
> Give every man thine ear, but few thy voice;   10
> Take each man's censure, but reserve thy judgement.
> Costly thy habit, as thy purse can buy,
> But not expressed in fancy; rich, not gaudy,
> For the apparel oft proclaims the man,
> And they in France of the best rank and station   15
> Are of a most select and generous chief in that.
> Neither a borrower nor a lender be,
> For loan oft loses both itself and friend,
> And borrowing dulls the edge of husbandry.
> This above all, to thine own self be true,   20
> And it must follow as the night the day
> Thou canst not then be false to any man.

1   **Give thy thoughts no tongue:**
       keep a close watch on what you say

2   **Nor any unproportioned thought his act:**
       if a thought crosses your mind, consider it carefully before acting

4   **Those friends thou hast, and their adoption tried:**
       those friends whose friendship you have tested

6-7   **do not dull thy palm ... unfledged courage:**
do not be too friendly with everyone you meet

8-9   **being in,/Bear 't that th' opposed may beware of thee:**
in a quarrel, behave in such a way that your enemy fear you

11   **Take each man's censure, but reserve thy judgement:**
consider each man's point of view but decide yourself

12   **Costly thy habit, as thy purse can buy:**
wear the clothes you can afford

14   **the apparel oft proclaims the man:**
clothes make the man by adding to his appearance

15-16   **they in France ... chief in that:**
the upper classes in France know how to dress well

19   **borrowing dulls the edge of husbandry:**
if you have to borrow money to live, you will never learn to live within your means

Speech 3

"To be, or not to be"

Background to the Speech

Hamlet, confronted with the thought of revenge on Claudius, has been given to fits of melancholy. He acknowledges to himself that he has "lost all mirth, foregone all customs of exercises". His whole attitude to life is one of depression. He sees the earth as "a sterile promontory". He looks at the sky and knows it is a "majestical roof fretted with golden fire" but in his present mood it is only "a foul and pestilent congregation of vapours".

At all times he searches for excuses for delaying his action of revenge and is delighted when a company of strolling Players arrives at Elsinore. He promises himself that his procrastination is only temporary and that he can use the Players to good account. He will have them present a murder play containing episodes which resemble those of the actual killing of his late father. He intends to observe his uncle closely during the performance and again promises himself "if he but blanch, I know my course". He sees in the play a solution to his doubts as to the king's guilt. He is aware that he has promised his father's ghost to take revenge but his excessive sensibility makes him delay: he must be sure.

Hamlet before the Crisis

As we look at Hamlet just before the crisis we need to probe more deeply into his mind: the soliloquy "to be or not to be" helps us see a man:

(a) torn by inner strife. He is confronted with an enormous problem to kill an anointed king and then to justify that deed to his mother and the world.

(b)   whose action of revenge is paralysed by his conscience and he is frustrated by the very thought of the task in front of him. It is for him not only the task of revenge against one man but an impossible feat of curing a degenerate world.

(c)   who seeks solace in escaping from his own personal suffering and heavy responsibility to a detached contemplation of the great issues of life: about death, eternity, suicide, immortality, religion and the source of life.

(d)   who himself is suffering from the sickness of life and he longs for death.

(e)   who is conscious of the "oppressor's wrongs", "the pangs of despised love", the "law's delay" and the "insolence of office".

(f)   who meditates deeply upon the undeserved sufferings of mankind, "the sling and arrows of outrageous fortune".

(g)   who sees in death a desirable end in itself, an end to all the "heartaches and thousand natural shocks".

(h)   who suffers from his own indecision about suicide. Death, he knows, can bring an end to his "weary life" but then there is the dread of something after death. His "conscience" is making a "coward" of him and he writhes under the agony of his own moral and intellectual scruples.

(i)   who is a man now faced with so many possibilities that his will is weakened and all enterprise for him has lost the name of action: his

> "native hue of resolution
> Is sicklied o'er with the pale cast of thought."

Speech 3: "To be, or not to be"

HAMLET

> To be, or not to be - that is the question:
> Whether 'tis nobler in the mind to suffer
> The slings and arrows of outrageous fortune
> Or to take arms against a sea of troubles
> And by opposing end them. To die, to sleep -   5
> No more - and by a sleep to say we end
> The heartache, and the thousand natural shocks
> That flesh is heir to. 'Tis a consummation
> Devoutly to be wished. To die, to sleep -
> To sleep - perchance to dream; ay, there's the rub,   10
> For in that sleep of death what dreams may come
> When we have shuffled off this mortal coil,
> Must give us pause. There's the respect
> That makes calamity of so long life.
> For who would bear the whips and scorns of time,   15
> Th' oppressor's wrong, the proud man's contumely
> The pangs of despised love, the law's delay,
> The insolence of office, and the spurns
> That patient merit of th' unworthy takes,
> When he himself might his quietus make   20
> With a bare bodkin? Who would fardels bear,
> To grunt and sweat under a weary life,
> But the dread of something after death,
> The undiscovered country, from whose bourn
> No traveller returns, puzzles the will,   25
> And makes us rather bear those ills we have
> Than fly to others that we know not of?
> Thus conscience does make cowards of us all,
> And thus the native hue of resolution
> Is sicklied o'er with the pale cast of thought,   30
> And enterprises of great pitch and moment

With this regard their currents turn awry
And lose the name of action. - Soft you now,
The fair Ophelia! - Nymph, in thy orisons
Be all my sins remembered.   35

3   **The slings and arrows of outrageous fortune:**
         the trials and tribulations of life

7   **The heartache, and the thousand natural shocks:**
         the sorrows and trials that we all have to endure

8-9   **'Tis a consummation/Devoutly to be wish:**
         it is the result that (I) dearly wished

10   **there's the rub:** this is the obstacle

12   **When we have shuffled off this mortal coil:**
         when we have ridden ourselves of all the problems that
         life brings

16   **the proud man's contumely:**
         the insolence of the proud man

18   **The insolence of office:**
         the over-bearing behaviour of those in authority

18-19   **the spurns/That patient merit of the unworthy takes:**
         the insults that we are expected to bear patiently

20   **When he himself might his quietus make:**
         when he can easily obtain peace by ending his life

21   **With a bare bodkin:** with a mere dagger

         Who would fardels bear:
         who would put up with the burdens of life

24-25   **The undiscovered country ... no traveller returns:**
         the after-life from the border of which nobody comes
         back

29-30   **the native hue of resolution ... the pale cast of thought:**
> too much serious thinking over an action makes the actual action difficult to perform

34-35   **Nymph, in thy orisons/Be all my sins remembered:**
> O beautiful maiden, ask God's forgiveness for my sins

Speech 4

"Now might I do it pat"

Claudius Alone

In Act III scene iii we have a picture of King Claudius, alone, and at prayer. Up to now he has never been alone and he has good reasons for this:

— He has murdered his own brother, the king.

— He has grabbed his throne and kingdom.

— He has married his wife.

— He has been an adulterer, murderer, usurper, and now he is king, with the need to sustain the appearance of innocence that is demanded: always to be cool and collected, always to be on the alert.

— Therefore it is necessary for him always to be in the company of those whom he has deceived and at the same always have his protecting bodyguard close at hand.

Claudius at Prayer

During the play scene by Hamlet's strolling players we hear Claudius give damning confirmation of his past crimes:

— He is now aware of his own guilt and we hear him cry aloud: "my offence is rank, it smells to heaven".

— He knows what his guilt is: it is the guilt of a "brother's blood".

— He writhes under the burden of remorse and tries to pray for forgiveness.

— But he is not prepared to forgo the fruits of his sins: he is determined to hold on to the crown, the queen and his ambition.

— He knows that forgiveness is impossible without repentance and that his bosom is still "black as death".

— He battles within himself for salvation and strives to pray, but he cannot; he is too hardened in his sins.

— He accepts the situation and decides "all may be well".

Hamlet's Golden Opportunity

Our interest all throughout the play is in the attitude of mind of Hamlet towards the fulfilment of his duty of revenge. And here we see him with a golden opportunity to translate his resolution for revenge into action. He has his sword at the ready and his enemy is alone and at prayer, with nobody to defend him:

— But it is an opportunity lost.

— Hamlet has delayed for far too long to turn back.

— Instead, once again, he searches for reasons not to take action.

— The reasons are not hard to find:

(a) To kill Claudius as he purges his soul is only to send him to heaven.

(b) To do that is not revenge but "hire and salary".

(c) Better to delay, to look for "a more horrid hent" and kill him when he is drunk, in a rage, in the incestuous pleasure of his bed, gaming, swearing, or engaged in some action that has not the "relish of salvation in it".

Turning Point of the Play

The loss of this opportunity and this soliloquy is the whole turning point of the play. The failure to take action here is the cause of all the deaths of Polonius, Rosencrantz, Guildenstern, Ophelia, the Queen, Laertes and Hamlet himself.

Speech 4: "Now might I do it pat"

HAMLET

           Now might I do it pat, now he is a-praying,
And now I'll do 't. And he goes to heaven,
And so am I revenged. That would be scanned.
A villain kills my father, and for that
I, his sole son, do this same villain send   5
To heaven.
Why, this is hire and salary, not revenge.
He took my father grossly, full of bread,
With all his crimes broad blown, as flush as May;
And how his audit stands, who knows save heaven?   10
But in our circumstance and course of thought,
'Tis heavy with him; and am I then revenged,
To take him in the purging of his soul,
When he is fit and seasoned for his passage?
No.   15
Up, sword, and know thou a more horrid hent,
When he is drunk asleep, or in his rage,
Or in th' incestuous pleasure of his bed,
At game a-swearing, or about some act
That has no relish of salvation in 't -   20
Then trip him, that his heels may kick at heaven,
And that his soul may be as damned and black
As hell, whereto it goes. My mother stays.
This physic but prolongs thy sickly days.

1   **Now might I do it pat:**
      I could do it just now

3   **That would be scanned:** people would conclude

7   **this is hire and salary, not revenge:**
      to kill a king at prayer is only rewarding him, not taking
      revenge on him

8   **He took my father grossly, full of bread:**
      he cruelly murdered my father, who was full of life

9   **With all his crimes broad blown:**
      with all his crimes well known by everyone

10   **how his audit stands, who knows save heaven:**
      only God knows how many sins he has committed

11-12 **But in our circumstance ... 'Tis heavy with him:**
      as far as we know, his punishment could be severe

13   **To take him in the purging of his soul:**
      to murder him just when he is repenting of his crimes

14   **When he is fit and seasoned for his passage:**
      when he is ready for his eternal reward (heaven)

16   **know thou a more horrid hent:**
      plan a more horrible opportunity to kill him

19-20 **some act/That has no relish of salvation in 'it:**
      a moment when you are engaged in a sinful deed

23   **My mother stays:** my mother is waiting for me

24   **This physic but prolongs thy sickly days:**
      this spiritually healthy state only prolongs the decisions
      for my horrible crime against you

Speech 5

"How all occasions do inform against me"

Background to the Speech

King Claudius has been plotting to rid himself of Hamlet and has arranged for Hamlet to go to England where he intends to have him killed. However, Hamlet escapes aboard a pirate vessel and lands in Denmark. There he see Fortinbras with 20,000 men marching over Danish territory. He looks at this young, tender Prince who has disciplined himself and his lawless band of resolutes and is invading foreign shores just for the sake of honour. The contrast between himself and Fortinbras strikes him to the core and once again he plunges into deep thought instead of action.

The Thoughts

(a) He sees in Fortinbras the qualities for action that he himself lacks: a young prince, with the capacity for leadership, driven forward by "spirit and divine ambition", prepared to risk his own death and the deaths of 20,000 men, because the honour of his country is at stake.

(b) He sees himself lacking this spirit and the self-indictment makes it all the more bitter, and he is aware of his own inactivity: his revenge is a "dull revenge".

(c) He is struck with shame at his own inability to act. He is convinced he has "cause" for taking revenge and the power to carry it through. "Sith I have cause, and will and strength and means/To do 't", but he knows too that he has failed.

(d) He probes deeply into himself and realises why he has so far failed: "thinking too precisely on the event", instead of plunging forward into action.

(e) He knows he is prompted to revenge by heaven and by hell but he lacks the "gall to make oppression bitter".

(f) He knows he has learnt little from his procrastination in the past and that his only action has been "bloody thoughts".

(g) But he also knows that he is not the same man:

> to stir without great argument
> to find quarrel in a straw
> to endanger the lives of 20,000 men
> for a fantasy, and trick of fame.

(h) All his probing, all his agony of shame, leads him to one direction:

> "from this time forth,
> my thoughts be bloody, or be nothing worth."

Justification for Hamlet

It is so easy to condemn Hamlet for his procrastination, but before we do so, it is but right to judge him by the standards of his age. It was a period of breaking-up of creeds and dilemmas of all kinds. It was an age that had to cope with major discussions about life, death, salvation and damnation. Such profound thoughts require arguments back and forth and all that needs the delay of time.

What can be said in Hamlet's favour is that he flings his whole being, his mind and his affections, into the trial of his soul's adventure on the road to revenge. His thoughts sap his whole resolution and made it ineffective but they sharpen his sense of right and wrong.

Speech 5: "How all occasions do inform against me"

HAMLET

          How all occasions do inform against me
And spur my dull revenge! What is a man,
If his chief good and market of his time
Be but to sleep and feed? A beast, no more.
Sure he that made us with such large discourse,   5
Looking before and after, gave us not
That capability and godlike reason
To fust in us unused. Now, whether it be
Bestial oblivion, or some craven scruple
Of thinking too precisely on th' event -   10
A thought which, quartered, hath but one part wisdom
And ever three parts coward - I do not know
Why yet I live to say, 'This thing's to do',
Sith I have cause, and will, and strength, and means
To do 't. Examples gross as earth exhort me.   15
Witness this army of such mass and charge,
Led by a delicate and tender prince,
Whose spirit, with divine ambition puffed,
Makes mouths at the invisible event,
Exposing what is mortal and unsure   20
To all that fortune, death, and danger dare,
Even for an eggshell. Rightly to be great
Is not to stir without great argument,
But greatly to find quarrel in a straw
When honour's at stake. How stand I then,   25
That have a father killed, a mother stained,
Excitements of my reason and my blood,
And let all sleep, while to my shame I see
The imminent death of twenty thousand men
That for a fantasy and trick of fame   30

Go to their graves like beds, fight for a plot
Whereon the numbers cannot try the cause,
Which is not tomb enough and continent
To hide the slain? O, from this time forth,
My thoughts be bloody, or be nothing worth!   35

1   **How all occasions do inform against me:**
        everything tells me I have failed to take revenge

5-8   **he that made us ... to fust in us unused:**
        God gave us the ability to speak, not to become mouldy
        through its lack of use

8-9   **whether it be/Bestial oblivion:**
        whether it is the forgetfulness of a beast

9   **some craven scruple:** some cowardly prick of conscience

14   **Sith I have cause:** since I have every reason

16   **Witness this army of such mass and charge:**
        look at this army made up of such large numbers and
        raised at such expense

18-19   **Whose spirit ... Makes mouths at the invisible event:**
        the spirit of the Prince makes him scorn the conse-
        quences of his actions

20-22   **Exposing what is mortal ... for an eggshell:**
        putting the lives of men at danger for a mere trifle

29-31   **twenty thousand men ... Go to their graves:**
        soldiers in battle, for an imaginary point of honour, will
        face death

33-34   **Which is not tomb enough ... To hide the slain:**
        the plot of ground for which they fight is not large
        enough to hold the dead bodies

Questions

1. "Polonius is a man of maxims." Discuss this point of view. What do you think of his precepts on conduct, friendship, quarrels, dress and loans? What do you think of him as a father?

2. What is your impression of Hamlet's character?

3. Give the substance of Hamlet's soliloquy "To or not to be".

4. "Hamlet is too noble for his surroundings. He is an idealist brought low in a world of horrible realities." Consider this description of the play and say how far you would accept it as an adequate summary.

Memorable Lines

I, i: "It harrows me with fear and wonder."

"This bodes some strange eruption to our state."

"A mote it is to trouble the mind's eye."

"The graves stood tenantless and the sheeted dead
Did squeak and gibber in the Roman streets."

"But look, the morn in russet mantle clad
Walks o'er the dew of yon high eastern hill."

I, ii: "to perserver
In obstinate condolement is a course
Of impious stubbornness."

"Frailty, thy name is woman."

"I'll speak to it though hell itself should gape
And bid me hold my peace."

I, iii: "Give thy thoughts no tongue,
Nor any unproportioned thought his act."

"Those friends thou hast, and their adoption tried,
Grapple them to thy soul with hoops of steel."

"Give every man thine ear, but few thy voice."

"Neither a borrower nor a lender be,
For loan oft loses both itself and friend."

                 "To thine own self be true,
And it must follow as the night the day,
Thou canst not then be false to any man."

"Do not as some ungracious parsons do,
Show me the steep and thorny way to heaven,
Whiles like a puffed and reckless libertine
Himself the primrose path of dalliance treads
And recks not his own rede."

I, iv: "It is a custom
More honoured in the breach than the observance."

"Something is rotten in the state of Denmark."

I, v: "Haste me to know 't, that I, with wings as swift
As meditation or the thoughts of love,
May sweep to my revenge."

"Thus was I ...
Cut off even in the blossoms of my sin,
Unhouseled, disappointed, unaneled,
No reckoning made, but sent to my account
With all my imperfections on my head."

" ... one may smile, and smile, and be a villain."

"There are more things in heaven and earth, Horatio,
Than are dreamt of in your philosophy."

"The time is out of joint. O cursed spite
That ever I was born to set it right!"

II, i: "By indirections find directions out."

II, ii: "brevity is the soul of wit."

"Though this be madness, yet there's a method in it."

"There is nothing either good or bad but thinking makes it so."

"What a piece of work is a man, how noble in reason, how infinite in faculties; in form and moving how express and admirable, in action how like an angel, in apprehension how like a god: the beauty of the world, the paragon of animals!"

"The play's the thing
Wherein I'll catch the conscience of the king."

III, i: "Whether 'tis nobler in the mind to suffer
The slings and arrows of outrageous fortune,
Or to take up arms against a sea of troubles,
And by opposing end them."

"In that sleep of death what dreams may come
When we have shuffled off this mortal coil,
Must give us pause."

"Bear the whips and scorns of time ...
The pangs of despised love ...
The insolence of office ...
To grunt and sweat under a weary life."

" ... conscience does make cowards of us all."

III, iv: " ... A murderer and a villain ... a vice of kings ... a cutpurse of the empire ... A king of shreds and patches."

"This is the very coinage of your brain."

" ... 'tis the sport to have the enginer
Hoist with his own petar."

IV, i: "There's a matter in these sighs, these profound heaves.
You must translate."

"My soul is full of discord and dismay."

IV, iii: "Diseases desperate grown
By desperate appliance are relieved,
Or not at all."

IV, v: "When sorrows come, they come not single spies,
But in battalions."

"There's such divinity doth hedge a king
That treason can but peep to what it would."

" ... where the offence is, let the great axe fall."

IV, vii: "You must not think
That we are made of stuff so flat and dull
That we can let our beard be shook with danger,
And think it pastime."

                   "love is begun by time ...
Time qualifies the spark and fire of it.
There lives within the very flame of love
A kind of wick or snuff that will abate it."

V, i: "I tell thee, churlish priest,
A ministering angel shall my sister be
When thou liest howling."

V, ii: "Our discretion sometimes serves us well
When our deep plots do pall, and that should learn us."

"There's a divinity that shapes our ends,
Rough-hew them how we will."

"There's a special providence in the fall of a sparrow."

**"Admired Miranda!
Indeed the top of admiration."**

*photogtaph on page 173
shows Estelle Kohler as Miranda
and Christopher Gable as Ferdinand*

A Glance at

THE TEMPEST

Date of the Play

The Tempest was written in or around the years 1610-1611. It certainly belongs to the late period of Shakespeare's productions and comes after *Othello, Hamlet, Macbeth, King Lear* and *Coriolanus.*

It was performed at the Court of James I and may have been written to celebrate the betrothal of James I's daughter, Princess Elizabeth, to the German Prince Frederick, Elector Palatine, in 1612.

Outline of the Play

Prospero and Miranda live on an enchanted tropical island. The island is occupied only by Caliban, a son of a witch, Sycorax. Prospero had been absorbed in the study of magic and had been deposed from his dukedom by his brother Antonio.

Prospero, with the aid of Ariel, batters a ship at sea, brings the voyagers ashore. Among them is the gallant son of the King of Naples.

The ship carried the King of Naples, Alonso and the usurping Duke of Milan and their respective retinues and they are ship-wrecked on another part of the island. These include Alonso, Sebastian, Antonio and Gonzalo. Ariel's music lulls the King asleep. Sebastian and Antonio plan to kill him but Ariel awakens the intended victim.

The courtiers, Stephano and Trinculo are shipwrecked on still another part of the island and together with Caliban they plan to kill Prospero and seize the island. Miranda and Ferdinand exchange vows of love. Alonso is saddened by the supposed death of his son.

Prospero presents Ferdinand and Miranda with a prenuptial pageant enacted by the spirits Iris, Ceres and Juno, nymphs and dancing reapers. The alert Ariel reports the plot to Prospero and he orders Ariel to punish them.

All the conspirators are finally brought into a charmed circle before Prospero's cell. Prospero reveals his real identity. He commands Antonio to restore his dukedom. He warns Sebastian against further plots. He reveals Ferdinand and Miranda to the whole group. He abjures his magic and gives Ariel his freedom.

A Romantic Drama

The play is one of the most imaginative, original and varied of Shakespeare's romantic dramas. The story takes place on an enchanted island on which Prospero and his beautiful daughter Miranda live. The island had been the abode of a witch called Sycorax and her son Caliban and our first impression of the island is that it is a barren, deserted place, uninhabitable and inaccessible, fit only for wolves and bears. But we soon hear of:

— fresh springs and fertile places.

— oak, pine, cedar and crab trees.

— a lawn of short grass in front of Prospero's cell.

— a grove of lime trees.

It is not a dull and dreary place but a magic island that seems to have risen up out of the tempestuous seas and is now a suitable place and background for people to:

— fall in love.

— learn to be cheerful in adversity.

— devote their lives to helping others.

— achieve peace of mind through reconciliation and tolerance.

Theme of the Play

The story of the play is based on a thin plot. It tells of the:

— estrangement of two brothers, Prospero and Antonio.

— resultant suffering caused by this estrangement.

— eventual harmony brought about by the forgiving nature of one brother, Prospero.

The problem of liberty is at the heart and centre of *The Tempest*:

(a) Caliban is aware of his rights and demands them but refuses to give service in return for these. He sees slavery in service.

(b) Ferdinand is the heir to the throne of Naples but on the enchanted island he is prepared to endure patiently his log-bearing tasks on behalf of Prospero.

(c) Miranda is the daughter of the all-powerful magician, Prospero, but she too is willing to give service on behalf of love: "I'll be your servant, whether you will or no".

(d) Ariel pines for freedom but to gain it he has to be diligent in the performance of his tasks for Prospero, night and day.

As the dramatist develops this theme we see the mind of Shakespeare at work. True liberty for him is:

— being cheerful in the face of disaster and calamity.

— the acceptance of service not to self but to others.

— being sensitive to the injustice done to others.

Selection of Memorable Speeches

(1) "Admired Miranda! Indeed the top of admiration!"
"I do not know one of my sex; no woman's face remember"
Act III, Scene i, lines 38-58.   (Ferdinand and Miranda)

(2)   "You fools! I and my fellows are ministers of Fate"
      Act III, Scene iii, lines 60-82.   (Ariel)

(3)   "Our revels now are ended"
      Act IV, Scene i, lines 148-163.   (Prospero)

(4)   "I have bedimm'd the noontide sun"
      Act V, Scene i, lines 41-57.   (Prospero)

(5)   "Be not afeard; the isle is full of noises"
      Act III, Scene ii, lines 130-138.   (Caliban)

Speech 1

"Admired Miranda! Indeed the top of admiration"

"I do not know one of my sex; no woman's face remember"

Background to the Speech

Prospero and his beautiful daughter, Miranda, now dwell on a tropical enchanted island. Twelve years before, Prospero had been Duke of Milan but he was too absorbed in the study of magic and the betterment of his own mind to take any interest in the administration of his country. His brother Antonio had no trouble in deposing him. He was aided by Alonso, King of Naples, who was an inveterate enemy of Prospero's, an enemy mostly because he had to pay tribute to Prospero. They put Prospero and his little daughter adrift in a boat, hoping that they would meet with disaster. But the boat arrived safely at the island occupied by Caliban, the orphan son of the wicked witch, Sycorax. In the past twelve years Miranda has grown in beauty. The only occupants of the island during this time have been Prospero, Miranda, Caliban, and Prospero's spirits of the air and water.

Prospero's former enemies have been attending the wedding of the Princess of Naples in Africa and are on their homeward journey across the sea. Prospero sends his servant Ariel to batter the ship and scatter the voyagers in groups about the island. One of the voyagers is Ferdinand, the son of the King of Naples. It is he who meets and falls in love with Miranda.

It was love at first sight and only natural that Prospero should fear "lest too light winning make the prize light". He pretends to frown upon the love affair and decides to put Ferdinand to the test:

(a) He makes him a prisoner.

(b) He manacles his neck and feet.

(c) For food and drink he is given sea-water, fresh brook musssels, withered roots and husks.

(d) He has the daily task of bearing heavy logs to Prospero's cell.

The Love Interest

The falling in love and the courtship of Ferdinand and Miranda is one of the great beauties of the play. It brings to the play charm and purity and the added attraction of suddenness: theirs is love at first sight but it is love based and built on mutual admiration and mutual sympathy:

(a) As soon as Miranda sees Ferdinand she tells her father "Believe me, sir, it carries a brave form".

(b) She is so attracted to him that she wants to call him "a thing divine".

(c) She openly acknowledges that he is the first man "that e'er I sighed for".

(d) Ferdinand also has no hesitation in expressing undying love for her: "I'll make you queen of Naples".

If love is to last, particularly if it is love at first sight, it has to have time to mature and develop. That demands from both lovers great strength of character. So now let us take a closer look at both of them.

A Closer Look at Miranda

(a) She is one of the most beautiful of Shakespeare's creations.

(b)   She is the only female in the play.

(c)   She is unique - at the opening of the play she knows only two human beings, her father and Caliban.

(d)   Her disposition is sweet and tender. When she hears of the intrigues and plots of her uncle Antonio and of their banishment from Milan, her only thought is of the trouble that she must have been to her father.

(e)   She has the delicacy of innocence and the purity of mind that has not been touched with the combats and contacts of daily living in crowded cities.

(f)   She has a lively personality and the capacity for quick, keen feeling and thinking. When she hears of the suffering of those in the storm-tossed vessel her first words are words of pity.

(g)   When she sees Ferdinand for the first time her emotion for him is fresh, natural, untouched by all the laws of convention or custom and unspoilt by artificiality.

(h)   There is no cunning about her love, no pretended bashfulness. She offers to become Ferdinand's wife long before he has the courage to ask her: "I am your wife, if you will marry me".

(i)   Her most outstanding characteristic is gentle compassion. She sees Ferdinand enduring his slavery on the island with grace and her womanly tenderness comes to the fore. She weeps and volunteers to carry his burdens for him: "If I'll bear your logs the while".

(j)   She knows her own qualities reasonably well: " my modesty ... the jewel in my dower" - "I prattle something too wildly".

(k)   She is above all a pure child of nature and her love for Ferdinand constitutes the play's great charm.

A Closer Look at Ferdinand

If Ferdinand is worthy to be a husband of the beautiful, innocent Miranda he must be a man of outstanding qualities:

(a)   He is handsome. As soon as Miranda looked at him she saw "a brave form ... a spirit ... a thing divine".

(b)   He is certainly a suitable match. He is heir to the kingdom of Naples and so a marriage between him and Miranda would be politically desirable: it would bring peace between Naples and Milan.

(c)   He is not a weak-kneed or effeminate man. Francisco gives us a beautiful picture of Ferdinand's courageous struggling for life in the heavy seas after the shipwreck.

(d)   His bravery, too, is seen in his drawing his sword in an effort to resist the power of Prospero, as soon as he arrived on the island.

But aside from these he has other qualities more in keeping with his part as an eligible suitor and future husband of Miranda:

(a)   He is affectionate - his first words on the island were words of affection for his father, from whom he has been separated by the storm at at sea. He pines for his father.

(b)   He is a sensitive person. When he heard Ariel's song his sensitive soul was moved by the song and the music of the island.

(c)   Like Miranda he is open and spontaneous in love. As soon as he sees Miranda, he sees a woman "so perfect ... so peerless". He had known many other young ladies but in ethereal beauty, in simplicity, in the grace of her deportment, and especially in the sincerity of her affections, Miranda outstrips all these ladies.

(d) He is fully aware of his princely state: he is the heir to the throne. But he has the humility and the strength of character to be willing to be Prospero's log-carrier in order to win Miranda's love: "The mistress which I serve quickens what's dead/And makes my labours pleasures".

(e) He is devoted to Miranda and unwilling to allow her to suffer pain on his behalf. She is prepared to carry logs for him, but he does not agree:

> "No, precious creature;
> I had rather crack my sinews, break my back,
> Than you should such dishonour undergo,
> While I sit lazy by!"

It is obvious that true love really exists between Miranda and Ferdinand and it is this love that brings about the reunion of the estranged brothers in the play. We are left with a picture of happiness and an optimistic outlook for the future of the world.

Listen to both of them as they declare openly the depth of their love for each other:

Speech 1: "Admired Miranda! Indeed the top of admiration!

"I do not know one of my sex; no woman's face remember"

FERDINAND

          Admired Miranda!
Indeed the top of admiration, worth
What's dearest to the world! Full many a lady
I have eyed with best regard, and many a time
Th' harmony of their tongues hath into bondage   5
Brought my too diligent ear; for several virtues
Have I liked several women; never any
With so full soul but some defect in her
Did quarrel with the noblest grace she owed,
And put it to the foil. But you, O you,   10
So perfect and so peerless, are created
Of every creature's best.

MIRANDA

          I do not know
One of my sex; no woman's face remember,
Save, from my glass, mine own; nor have I seen
More that I may call men than you, good friend, 15
And my dear father. How features are abroad
I am skilless of; but, by my modesty
(The jewel in my dower), I would not wish
Any companion in the world but you;
Nor can imagination form a shape,   20
Besides yourself, to like of. But I prattle
Something too wildly, and my father's precepts
I therein do forget.

2-3   worth/What's dearest to the world:
Ferdinand looks upon Miranda as the best person in all
the world

3-4   Full many a lady/I have eyed with best regard:
I have looked at many ladies and had the highest
opinion of them

5-6   Th' harmony of their tongue ... my too diligent ear:
when I heard them speak I was so attracted to them that
I listened with full attention

8-9   some defect in her ... the noblest grace she owed:
some blemish or failing destroyed all her charm

10   put it to the foil: spoilt it

13-14 no woman's face ... from my glass, mine own:
the only woman's face I have seen is my own and that
was in my mirror

16-17 How features are abroad/I am skilless of:
I do not know what other men look like

17-18 my modesty/(The jewel in my dower):
my modesty is the best gift I bring to our relationship

20-21 Nor can imagination form a shape ... to like of:
I cannot imagine what other men look like

21   I prattle: I am talking like a child

Speech 2

"You fools: I and my fellows are ministers of Fate"

Ariel's Power

According to popular belief in Shakespeare's day the power of a spirit was supposed to be restricted to that part of the country where he/she resided. This is not so in the case of Ariel: his power is without limit:

(a) He has the power of all the elemental spirits amd therefore the powers of the elements.

(b) He can strike frighteningly like lightning.

(c) He is equally at home on sea, on land or in fire.

(d) His power has the swiftness of thought.

(e) He is a spirit of the highest order.

(f) He is like a bird: he can fly, swim, ride on the curled clouds, and sing songs.

Ariel's Character

These powers and talents could make us assume that Ariel is an abstraction, an imaginary creature, existing only in the mind of the dramatist. But Ariel is more than that:

(a) He is not an abstraction, but a real, living character, with a definite purpose in the play.

(b) He is the spiritual agent of Prospero, responsible for carrying out many duties himself but also for issuing orders to the other spirits of Prospero's household.

(c) He is active and zealous in the performance of all the tasks his master gives him.

(d) He is respectful and dutiful towards his master and carries out without question each least wish of Prospero's, quickly and strictly to the letter.

(e) He is on good terms with his master, yet, like a normal human being, he can become moody, ungrateful and forgetful of all that Prospero has done for him.

(f) He is sensitive to his master's moods and angry moments and is quick to react to them.

(g) When he is moody himself, particularly in his desire for freedom, he is too rarefied a spirit to continue long in sulking like a spoilt child.

Ariel's Music

When we consider anything that relates to Ariel, we must remember that we are on an enchanted island and, for the purpose of the play, keep our minds open to temporary belief in the power of Ariel's magic, almost the way a child does when listening to a fairy tale. This belief helps us appreciate the charm of the romantic drama. Magic in itself can be so attractive and the magical power of Ariel's music plays an important part in the play. By means of music, Ariel:

— leads Ferdinand from the seashore to Prospero's cell, where he meets Miranda.

— lulls Alonso, Gonzalo and the others to sleep and awakens Gonzalo just before Antonio and Sebastian plan to murder the sleeping king.

— obstructs the conspiracy of Caliban, Stephano and Trinculo against the life of Prospero.

Ariel's music is therefore of dramatic importance in the very structure of the play, at one time furthering the development of the plot, at another, delaying the action for a dramatic reason. It can also be a joy in itself: when Ariel at long last is given his long-desired freedom he sings a song of rapturous joy.

Ariel - A Spirit of Authority

Part of Ariel's responsibility is to deal with three evil men who have sinned against Prospero:

(a)   Alonso has been guilty of a crime against Prospero. He has been an enemy of the Duke and joined forces with Antonio in removing Prospero from his rightful position.

(b)   Antonio had deposed his own brother and had also drawn Sebastian into the plot, making him an accomplice.

In Speech 2 we see Ariel dealing with these three men:

(a)   They are all three powerful men in their own rights and even now fully armed.

(b)   But Ariel is in complete control of the situation. He shows no sign of fear.

(c)   He tells them that he and his "fellow ministers are invulnerable", that their swords are useless against him: "You may as well wound the loud winds" or try "to kill the still closing waters".

(d)   He warns them that he has already used his powers against them in causing the shipwreck.

(e)   He emphasises the reasons for his actions: their foul deeds.

(f)   He threatens them with "lingering perdition worse than any death" unless they change their evil ways.

(g)   He offers them his peace-offering: they can have peace of mind but only on one condition: through repentance - heart-felt sorrow and "a clear life".

Speech 2: "You fools: I and my fellows are ministers of Fate"

[Alonso, Sebastian, etc., draw their swords.]

ARIEL

You fools: I and my fellows
Are ministers of Fate. The elements,
Of whom your swords are tempered, may as well
Wound the loud winds, or with bemocked-at stabs
Kill the still-closing waters, as diminish   5
One dowle that's in my plume. My fellow ministers
Are like invulnerable. If you could hurt,
Your swords are now too massy for your strengths
And will not be uplifted. But remember
(For that's my business to you) that you three   10
From Milan did supplant good Prospero;
Exposed unto the sea, which hath requit it,
Him and his innocent child; for which foul deed
The powers, delaying, not forgetting, have
Incensed the seas and shores, yea, all the creatures,   15
Against your peace. Thee of thy son, Alonso,
They have bereft; and do pronounce by me
Lingering perdition (worse than any death
Can be at once) shall step by step attend
You and your ways; whose wraths to guard you from,   20
Which here, in this most desolate isle, else falls
Upon your heads, is nothing but heart's sorrow
And a clear life ensuing.

1-2   **I and my fellows/Are ministers of Fate:**
I and my fellow spirits carry out the commands of
Prospero

2-3   **The elements,/Of whom your swords are tempered:**
the steel of your swords is hardened but useless against
the winds

4   **bemocked-at stabs:**
your attacks on the ocean are laughable

5-6   **diminish/One dowle that's in my plume:**
break even one portion of the feathers in my wings

6-7   **My fellow ministers/Are like invulnerable:**
the spirits that work along with me are also untouchable

8   **Your swords are now too massy:**
your swords are now too heavy

11   **From Milan did supplant good Prospero:**
(you) expelled Prospero from Milan by underhand
means

16-17   **Thee of thy son, Alonso,/They have bereft:**
Alonso, they have robbed you of your son

Speech 3

"Our revels now are ended"

Background to the Speech

Prospero, as a wise and caring father, has put his future son-in-law's expressions of love for Miranda to the test and is now satisfied about the sincerity of this love. He releases Ferdinand from his log-bearing tasks and blesses the betrothal of the lovers. To celebrate the occasion he arranges a prenuptial pageant with his nymphs dancing and rejoicing at a contract of true love. Just as the pageant is well under way, it suddenly stops: Prospero remembers the foul conspiracy against his own life by Caliban and his associates. He is vexed and sorely troubled. He wishes to be alone, in order to think about the meaning of life and tells the lovers to retire into his cell.

A Look at Prospero

In order that we may not be like Ferdinand, "moved" and "dismayed" at this sudden change in the attitude and behaviour of Prospero. We must sit back, pause and consider the character of the man himself. It will also help us to understand the importance of this speech:

(a) He has been an affectionate father with a sensitive heart. His life has been devoted to the care of his daughter and it is natural that he should derive such joy in her attachment to such a fine person as Ferdinand.

(b) He has given a lot of thought to the sacredness of the marriage vow and shows a full understanding of the worth of true love.

(c) As Duke of Milan he had been a care-free, retiring student, unwilling to accept his full responsibility of governing his country. But now he is the wise philosopher, with a keen sense of all his duties, as father and as ruler of the island.

(d) In his dedication to the bettering of his own mind he had neglected his duties to the State and its people. But misfortune has taught him that the neglect had brought about his own misfortune.

(e) As Duke of Milan he had been too generous, too trusting, with too much unlimited faith in others and it had cost him his dukedom. He has learnt now when to be strong, when to be tender, when to be stern and when to forgive.

(f) He is not a colourless, passionless character but a person of strong feelings, a man who has given considerable thought to the meaning of life. To him the prenuptial festivities are tinged with the sadness of a conspiracy and it brings deep and serious thoughts into his mind.

His Serious Thoughts

Prospero has come to the conclusion that:

(a) all life is transitory and not an end in itself.

(b) towers, palaces, temples and the world itself will one day "dissolve" and "leave not a rack behind".

(c) this life is but a preparation for the life to come: "we are such stuff as dreams are made on".

Such serious thoughts are the thoughts of a man of strong personality. It is with the strength of his personality that we should approach Speech 3.

Speech 3: "Our revels are ended"

PROSPERO

           Our revels now are ended. These our actors,
As I foretold you, were all spirits and
Are melted into air, into thin air;
And, like the baseless fabric of this vision,
The cloud-capped towers, the gorgeous palaces,   5
The solemn temples, the great globe itself,
Yea, all which it inherit, shall dissolve,
And, like this insubstantial pageant faded,
Leave not a rack behind. We are such stuff
As dreams are made on, and our little life   10
Is rounded with a sleep. Sir, I am vexed.
Bear with my weakness: my old brain is troubled.
Be not disturbed with my infirmity.
If you be pleased, retire into my cell
And there repose. A turn or two I'll walk   15
To still my beating mind.

1   **Our revels now are ended:**
       our entertainment, festivities, are now over

6-7   **the great globe itself,/Yea, all which it inherit:**
       the world and all who inhabit it

10-11 **our little life/Is rounded with a sleep:**
       our short lives are rounded off with the sleep of death

11-12 **I am vexed./Bear with my weakness:**
       I am angry, annoyed; be patient with me

15   **A turn or two I'll walk:**
       I will go for a short walk

16   **To still my beating mind:** to calm my troubled mind

Speech 4

"I have bedimmed the noontide sun"

A Fairytale

The Tempest is a fairytale and like a good tale it provides us with wonderful flights into the realm of fairyland. But even in this fairyland there are men who have committed horrible crimes and who are still plotting against the lives of their fellowmen. A fairytale cannot end with their success: it must end on a happy note and give a picture of a brave new world where enmities cease and there is hope for the future.

— Prospero is at the height of his power and he uses this power for good. He charms the entire company into his magic circle and pardons all those who have sinned against him.

— Alonso recognises the part he played in the crime, feels remorse and his remorse leads him to repentance.

— Antonio does not feel remorse, and in spite of his brother's pardon, remains hardened in sullen spite.

— Sebastian was a man who was easily led into sin by others and Prospero is sorry for him but at the same time warns him about his future actions.

— Caliban is repentant and promises to be wise hereafter and seek grace. He merits Prospero's forgiveness.

There is happiness, too, in store for others:

— The lovers had looked forward to the fulfilment of their love in marriage: we hear of the plans for their marriage in Naples.

— Ariel has given long and faithful service to Prospero and for this he is given his freedom, but not without a pull at the heart-strings of his master: "I shall miss thee. But yet thou shalt have freedom".

— Prospero is also finally united in love and harmony with the brother who had plotted against his life.

So our fairytale, like all good fairytales, ends happily.

The Final Curtain

Before the final curtain comes down on this romantic fairytale we are given a last glimpse of Prospero and his intentions:

(a) We see him as a dignified, self-possessed man of character.

(b) He has put an end to all the foul conspiracies and forgiven all.

(c) Twelve years of solitude and self-sacrifice on the island have given him a new philosophy of life: he desires penitence, not revenge ("the rarer action is in virtue than in vengeance").

(d) He has had unlimited power to:

  — bedim "the noontide sun".

  — call forth "the mutinous winds".

  — give fire to "the dread rattling thunder".

  — rift "Jove's stout oak with his own bolt".

  — shake "the strong-based promontory".

  — uproot "the pine and cedar".

  — open graves and waken the dead.

(e) It is a solemn moment for Prospero. He renounces all earthly thoughts and pleasures, all petty personal motives and mean concerns of men and with great dignity he is willing to abjure his magic art and break his staff.

Perhaps in this final picture of Prospero we can see Shakespeare himself. *The Tempest* is one of his final plays and perhaps here he sees himself in retirement, returning to the Stratford that he loved so dearly, spending his days there to the betterment of his mind.

Speech 4: I have bedimmed the noontide sun

PROSPERO

> I have bedimmed
> The noontide sun, called forth the mutinous winds,
> And 'twixt the green sea and the azured vault
> Set roaring war; to the dread rattling thunder
> Have I given fire and rifted Jove's stout oak   5
> With his own bolt; the strong-based promontory
> Have I made shake and by the spurs plucked up
> The pine and cedar; graves at my command
> Have waked their sleepers, oped, and let 'em forth
> By my so potent art. But this rough magic   10
> I here abjure; and when I have required
> Some heavenly music (which even now I do)
> To work mine end upon their senses that
> This airy charm is for, I'll break my staff,
> Bury it certain fathoms in the earth,   15
> And deeper than did ever plummet sound
> I'll drown my book.

1-2   **I have bedimmed/The noontide sun:**
      I have cast a cloud over the sun at noontime

3-4   **'twixt the green sea ... vault/Set roaring war:**
      created storms between the seas and the light blue sky

4-5   **to the dread rattling thunder/Have I given fire:**
      I have added lightning to the terrifying thunder

5   **rifted Jove's stout oak:**
      uprooted Jupiter's, the king of the gods' strong oak tree

6-7   **the strong-based promontory/Have I made shake:**
      I have shaken the solid headlands

8-9   **graves .../Have waked their sleepers, oped:**
        graves have opened and the dead have walked at my
        command

10   **By my so potent art:**
        by my all-powerful magic

10-11   **this rough magic/I here abjure:**
        I lay aside, renounce, my magic art

14   **I'll break my staff:**
        I will destroy the outward sign of my authority as a
        magician

17   **I'll drown my book:** I will throw away my book of charms

Speech 5

"Be not afeard: the isle is full of noises"

A Look at Caliban

Caliban is a creature deformed in mind and body yet something of the spirit of the island has gone into his character. It is Caliban who utters this speech which is one of the most poetical passages in the play. Before we read the speech, let us look at the man himself:

(a) Physically, he is ugly and repulsive, uncontrolled, uncouth and wild.

(b) He curses at all times in the performance of his menial tasks for Prospero.

(c) He is not held in high esteem by anyone. Even the clown Trinculo considers him "a most credulous monster ... most perfidious ... a most ridiculous monster ... a howling monster."

(d) Morally, he is depraved and vicious, a monster, resembling nothing in the range of imaginative literature.

(e) He is the entire product of Shakespeare's imagination - the wildest, the most abstracted of his creations.

(f) He is the essence of physical grossness but yet there is not a particle of vulgarity in him.

(g) He is half-demon, half-brute but beneath this ugly exterior he is keenly alive to the charm of music and the beauty of the island.

(h) He has many qualities that raise him above our contempt, particularly his knowledge of every fertile inch of the island:

— He knows where the best springs and berries are.

— He knows where jays build their nests.
— He can instruct "how to snare the nimble marmoset".
— He can bring you to "clustering filberts".
— He can clothe all commonplace things in highly poetical language.

A Fitting Close

As we come to the end of this glance at *The Tempest* it is fitting that we have a final look at the island and what better way than by listening to the magic of Caliban's words:

Speech 5: "Be not afeard: the isle is full of noises"

CALIBAN

> Be not afeard: the isle is full of noises,
> Sounds and sweet airs that give delight and hurt not.
> Sometimes a thousand twangling instruments
> Will hum about mine ears; and sometime voices
> That, if I then had waked after long sleep,   5
> Will make me sleep again; and then, in dreaming,
> The clouds methought would open and show riches
> Ready to drop upon me, that, when I waked,
> I cried to dream again.

1   **Be not afeared:** do not be afraid

3   **twangling instruments:** musical instruments making metallic sounds

Questions

1. Who are the three men of sin? What sins had they committed?

2. Ariel points out the atonement the three men of sin must make. What is it? If they fail in this, he warns them of their punishment. What is it?

3. What is Prospero's attitude towards vengeance?

4. How powerful is Prospero as a magician?

Suggestions for Further Work on *The Tempest*

Note that in context questions it is important to give the following details:

(a) The name of the speaker.

(b) In what circumstances the words were spoken. To whom?

(c) Any important bearing the words have upon the plot.

(d) Any light thrown upon the character of the speaker or about whom it is spoken.

(e) Note any unusual words and suggest a meaning.

1.   The winds did sing it to me and the thunder,
      That deep and dreadful organ-pipe, pronounced
      the name of Prosper.

2.   Graves at my command
      Have waked their sleepers, oped, let 'em forth
      By my so potent art.

Memorable Lines

II, i: "He receives comfort like cold porridge."

"He's winding up the watch of his wit; by and by it will strike."

"The air breathes upon us here most sweetly."

II, ii: "Misery acquaints a man with strange bedfellows."

III, i: "I had rather crack my sinews, break my back,
Than you should such dishonour undergo
While I sit lazy by."

          "Full many a lady
I have eyed with best regard, and many time
The harmony of their tongues hath into bondage
Brought my too diligent ear."

          "My modesty,
(The jewel of my dower)."

III, ii: "The isle is full of noises,
Sounds and sweet airs that give delight and hurt not.

Sometimes a thousand twangling instruments
Will hum about mine ears; and sometime voices
That, if I then had waked after long sleep
Would make me sleep again."

III, iii: "The winds did sing it to me; and the thunder,
That deep and dreadful organ-pipe, pronounced
The name of Prosper."

IV, i: "All thy vexations
Were but my trials of thy love, and thou
Hast strangely stood the test."

"If thou dost break her virgin-knot before
All sanctimonious ceremonies may
With full and holy rite be ministered,
No sweet aspersion shall the heaven let fall
To make this contract grow; but barren hate,
Sour-eyed disdain, and discord shall bestrew
The union of your bed."

                "The strongest oaths are straw
To the fire i' the blood."

                "We are such stuff
As dreams are made on, and our little life
Is rounded with a sleep."

V, i: "His tears run down his beard, like winter's drops
From eaves of reeds."

                "The rarer action is
In virtue than in vengeance."

                "The charm dissolves apace;
And as the morning steals upon the night,
Melting the darkness, so their rising senses
Begin to chase the ignorant fumes that mantle
Their clearer reason."

                "O brave new world
That has such people in 't."